Addressing Gender Differences in Young Adolescents

Deborah A. Butler, Wabash College and

M. Lee Manning, Old Dominion University

Association for Childhood Education International
17904 Georgia Ave., Ste. 215, Olney, MD 20832
1-800-423-3563 • http://www.udel.edu/bateman/acei

Anne W. Bauer, Editor / Director of Publications
Bruce Herzig, Assistant Editor

Photographs
Pages 8, 44, 78, © 1998, Robert Finken
Page 22, © 1998, Harry Cutting
Page 114, © 1998, Marilyn Nolt

Copyright © 1998, Association for Childhood Education International
17904 Georgia Ave., Ste. 215, Olney, MD 20832

Library of Congress Cataloging-in-Publication Data
Butler, Deborah A.
    Addressing gender differences in young adolescents / Deborah
Butler and M. Lee Manning
        p.   cm.
    Includes bibliographical references.
    ISBN 0-87173-144-4 (paperback)
    1. Teenagers--Education (Middle school)--United States. 2. Sex
differences in education--United States. 3. Sex differences
(Psychology) in adolescence--United States. 4. Sex discrimination
in education--United States. I. Manning, M. Lee. II. Title.
    LB1623.B88   1998
    306.43'2--dc21   98-22352
                                                                              CIP

Table of Contents

Prologue

The current interest in recognizing and addressing the gender differences that characterize young adolescents suggests a need to focus on how gender differences affect teaching-learning situations, and on how middle level school educators can address these differences. "Gender" as a term represents the differences between masculinity and femininity—the thoughts, feelings, and behavior identified as either female or male. While many similarities exist between females and males, differences (many of which result from societal teachings and expectations) also exist for which educators should plan gender-responsive educational experiences. Likewise, educators have a responsibility to clarify stereotypical beliefs about females and males.

Several factors provide the foundation for *Addressing Gender Differences in Young Adolescents*. First, middle level educators need to consider gender (both female and male) in terms of differences to be understood, appreciated, and addressed. Second, educators, especially middle level educators, should choose textbooks and other curricular materials carefully to ensure accurate portrayals of females and males. Third, middle level school educators should examine daily educational practices to uncover any gender inequities, whether conscious or unconscious.

We also believe that educators will want to avoid stereotypes that define females and males in narrow roles. Both genders learn gender stereotypes through games they play, television programs showing boys in active roles and females in passive roles, and educators' expectations of gender-specific behaviors of females and males. Consequently, educators face a significant challenge. In their efforts to address gender diversity, middle level educators need to provide teaching-learning experiences that reflect a recognition and an understanding of gender.

In *Addressing Gender Differences in Young Adolescents* we will strive to explain what gender differences are, how gender differences affect learning, how both girls and boys need their gender differences addressed, and how gender differences can be addressed. Chapter 1, "Gender and Young Adolescents," represents a "call to professional action" by encouraging middle level educators to accept the professional responsibility to understand and address gender differences. Chapter 2, "Gender Differences in Young Adolescents: Research and Literature," examines selected research studies and scholarly literature on gender differences and considers its implications for gender-responsive school environments and educational experiences. Chapter 3 focuses on "Gender Equity and the Middle Level School Concept," showing how gender and gender issues can be threaded into essential middle level school concepts such as teacher advisories, exploratories, and positive school environments. Chapter 4, "Gender and the Middle Level School Curriculum," shows how gender, gender differences, and gender concerns can be reflected in the middle level school curriculum. Chapter 5 provides a look at "Additional Sources of Information."

Perceptive middle level educators realize that many more changes are long overdue.

Advocates of gender-equitable and gender-responsive middle level schools readily recognize that considerable progress has been achieved during the last decade or so. Still, perceptive middle level educators realize that many more changes are long overdue—changes affecting attitudes toward girls and boys, curricular and instructional materials, and teaching practices. Several factors suggest the future for gender-equitable and gender-responsive educational experiences looks promising. Gender and gender differences are increasingly addressed in the research and literature, more organizations and publishing houses are releasing publications on providing gender-equitable teaching and learning experiences, and more educators are realizing that educational experiences should be planned and implemented for both girls and boys. With an enhanced understanding of gender and the need for gender equity, the 21st century can be an ideal time to meet the needs of all young adolescents—both girls and boys.

Deborah Butler
Wabash College
M. Lee Manning
Old Dominion University

Part One: Gender, Young Adolescents, and Research

Chapter 1
Gender and Young Adolescents

*I*n recent years, differences associated with gender have been increasingly recognized and reflected in educational experiences. Researchers have documented the need for educators to recognize gender differences and to offer equitable responses to the learning and developmental needs of both boys and girls. Educators at all levels have a professional responsibility to address the individualized needs of both girls and boys, rather than catering toward only one gender. We believe that middle schools have perhaps an even greater responsibility to provide gender-equitable education responses because young adolescents are at an impressionable age—a time when they are developing gender identities and self-esteem, attitudes toward gender and society, and attitudes toward life. Effective middle schools have various programs to assist educators, library media specialists, and guidance counselors in addressing the needs of both genders. A positive learning environment, adviser-advisee programs, and exploratory programs are responses that have the potential for providing learning experiences that reflect the needs of both girls and boys.

While some educators might think gender equity exists in middle schools today, recent research suggests full gender equity has not been achieved among middle school girls and boys. In *Addressing Gender Difference in Young Adolescents*, we call attention to gender differences in young adolescents and encourage educators to provide gender-equitable educational experiences.

The Need for Gender Equity—Both Girls and Boys

The Women's Educational Equity Act (WEEA) defines gender equity as a set of actions, attitudes, and assumptions that provide opportunities and create expectations about individuals, *regardless of gender*. In a gender-equitable environment, females and males have an equal chance at:

- learning, regardless of the subject
- preparing for future education, jobs, and careers
- high expectations
- developing, achieving, and learning
- equitable treatment and outcomes in school and beyond (Women's Educational Equity Act, 1997).

Several other books and reports have called attention to how schools often cheat girls. During the early years of school, for example, girls score ahead or equal to boys on almost all standardized measures of achievement and psychological well-being. By graduation time, however, they score lower. Also, girls receive less active instruction, endure sexual harassment at increasing rates, suffer from declining self-esteem, and feel programmed for specific occupations and professions (American Association of University Women, 1992; "Education and Gender," 1994; Orenstein, 1994; Sadker & Sadker, 1994).

Of course, neither gender should be slighted—we believe that the need for gender equity also extends to boys who experience gender bias. Due to their gender, some boys rise to the top of the class, while others fall to the bottom. Labeled as problems in need of special control or assistance, boys are more likely to fail a course, miss promotion, or drop out of school. Their misbehavior results in more and harsher penalties (e.g., school suspensions and corporal punishment). Prone to take risks, they jeopardize both their academic future and their lives due to accident, suicide, and homicide. Because boys' educational failures are so visible and public, schools invest extra resources on their behalf, yet catastrophic results continue (Sadker & Sadker, 1994).

Sadker and Sadker (1994) called for gender equity for boys and summarized their position as such:

Until gender equity becomes a value promoted in every aspect of school, boys, as victims of their own miseducation, will grow up to be troubled men; they will be saddened by unmet expectations, unable to communicate with women as equals, and unprepared for modern life. (Sadker & Sadker, 1994, p. 225)

The Early Adolescence Developmental Period:
A Crucial Time for Gender Equity and Fairness

The early adolescence developmental period is a critical time for providing educational experiences that reflect gender. Middle school educators face significant daily challenges because this developmental period is so critical. During this crucial developmental period, young adolescents build self-esteem and mold gender identities, form opinions of others, and make close friends and social networks. They also develop a sense of justice and a perception of fairness—an overall sense of how people should be treated. Young adolescents need educational experiences that help them form positive opinions of the other gender, as well as their own. The self-esteem and gender identity they establish in this period may last a lifetime. Young adolescents' perceptions of gender differences and their opinions of others' perceptions play significant roles in their degree of self-worth and self-image.

At the same time that young adolescents are developing opinions of themselves and their gender, they are also forming opinions of others and making close friends. The individual's need for belonging and acceptance reaches in-

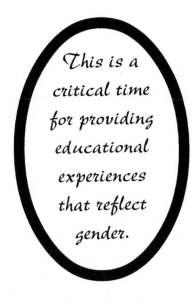

This is a critical time for providing educational experiences that reflect gender.

creased levels during the transition from childhood to adolescence. An educational environment that provides gender-responsive experiences contributes to worthy gender identities, positive self-esteem, and the formation of positive opinions of others and their differences. Such positive opinions can be formed when young adolescents work in cooperative learning or other small groups, as is discussed in Chapters 3 and 4.

Research (Manning, 1993) shows the importance of friendships to young adolescents. While young adolescents know other-gender students who are potential friends, they too often form friendships along gender lines due to either sexism, stereotypical mindsets, or the belief that gender is the most significant determining factor when selecting friends.

Young adolescents' psychosocial and cognitive development determines their perception of how others should be treated. They place importance on a sense of justice, a perception of fairness, and an overall understanding of how both genders should be treated. As young adolescents continue to develop, their sense of fair play and justice grows. Young adolescents often voice concerns about the fairness of situations, about injustices perpetrated on a group of people, or, perhaps, the ill treatment teachers and parents inflict upon young people (Manning, 1994). During this critical time, young adolescents should be encouraged to develop a sense of respect for both genders. As their socialization increases during this period, others are being considered as possible friends, and opinions of the other gender are being formed.

One final reason we feel the early adolescence developmental period is a crucial time for gender equity and fairness is that young adolescents become capable of engaging in social analysis, making judgments regarding personal and social behaviors, and developing a sense of morality and ethical behavior. Since some young adolescents might still be thinking in concrete terms while others have advanced to abstract thought, it is imperative that they be considered as individuals. Those who are abstract thinkers can form a basis for their own judgments, think through ethical and moral situations, and participate in social analysis of how and why people treat others as they do. The three processes correspond closely with how young adolescents perceive sexism, bias, and unjust treatment. Teaching young adolescents about the effects of sexism, discrimination, and unjust treatment of individuals has the potential for influencing learners' analysis of social situations and for influencing learners' developing sense of moral and ethical behavior.

Rationale for *Addressing Gender Differences in Young Adolescents*

Developmental and educational research, scholarly writings, and books in the popular press reveal how girls and boys have been socialized by the media, parents, the greater community, peers, and society as a whole to think differently and perceive school-related issues (such as motivation and perceptions of success) differently. Similarly, teachers often provide gender-specific educational and social experiences that contribute to this gender-related schism.

As Chapter 2 points out, research on gender differences has focused on development, proposed that socialization has powerful effects on girls' and boys' gender-related perceptions, and revealed interesting and informative findings. Because of this research, professional educators have become increasingly interested in gender and gender-related concerns.

Referring to how schools treat girls, Myra and David Sadker (1994) called girls "second-class educational citizens" (p. 1). A professor once showed his gender-bias in class as he spoke of a "girl student" he had taught the previous semester. He remarked on her tremendous intelligence and writing ability and finished by saying, "All those brains wasted on a girl." The class was left with no doubt about his perceptions of females.

Many schools shortchange girls, which results in loss of self-esteem, decline in achievement, and a narrowing of career options. Less than a century ago, girls' lower performance on standardized tests, their loss of self-esteem, and their under-enrollment in higher education and professional schools were not considered problems. In fact, "girls and schools seemed a match made in heaven" (Sadker & Sadker, 1994, p. 215). Schools shortchange boys, as well. Boys also had educational problems—many did not stay in school long enough to graduate and were termed "grade repeaters" and "retarded" (Sadker & Sadker, 1994, p. 215). Believing the Sadkers to be correct in their observations, we contend in *Addressing Gender Differences in Young Adolescents* that middle school educators need to take advantage of middle school concepts (such as adviser-advisee programs, exploratory programs, and positive school environments) to provide gender-equitable curricular and instructional experiences, and school environments that address the needs of both genders.

We believe that one gender should not be neglected at the expense of the other—both genders deserve middle schools that treat them fairly and equitably. Therefore, we have written this publication to help middle school educators recognize gender differences and similarities; understand how gender affects learning and development; provide gender-fair curricular, instructional, and environmental experiences for both girls and boys; and take advantage of essential middle school concepts (such as adviser-advisee and exploratory programs) to incorporate gender into all aspects of the middle school program. Such a rationale seems appropriate since, as Sadker and Sadker (1994) wrote, "the transition from elementary to middle school may be the most damaging period of a girl's young life" (p. 78). This transition can be equally damaging to boys.

Potential Education Issues for Girls and Boys

Authors in the popular press also offer insights for middle school educators. These authors include Myra and David Sadker, Lyn Mikel Brown and Carol Gilligan, Barrie Thorne, Mary Pipher, Peggy Orenstein, and various authors writing for the American Association of University Women. These writers, more than academic researchers, attempt to reach a general audience and try to convey the importance of considering gender and gender concerns. Their areas of interest include: 1) gender inequities in educational experiences for girls and boys, and the clear need to rectify previous and present practices and policies; 2) gender differences in the development of females and males and how both genders are socialized to perceive and behave in gender-specific terms; and 3) actual ways schools can provide educational experiences reflecting gender.

Myra and David Sadker called attention to these gender inequities in their book *Failing at Fairness: How America's Schools Cheat Girls* (1994). During the early years of school, for example, girls score ahead or equal to boys on almost all standardized measures of achievement and psychological well-being. By graduation time, however, they score lower. Also, girls in all grades receive less active instruction, endure sexual harassment at increasing rates, undergo declines in self-esteem, and feel programmed for specific occupations and professions (Sadker & Sadker, 1994).

In another excellent book, *Meeting at the Crossroads: Women's Psychology and Girls' Development*, Lyn Mikel Brown and Carol Gilligan (1992) raised significant questions about the relationship between women's psychological development and the society and cultures in which women live. Middle school educators should be interested in Brown's and Gilligan's assertion that for over a century "the edge of adolescence" (p. 2) has been a time of heightened psychological risk for girls. Mary Pipher (1994), in *Reviving Ophelia*, discussed the destructive nature of young women dressing "older," experimenting with alcohol and other drugs, and engaging in sexual activity. Peggy Orenstein, in *SchoolGirls: Young Women, Self-Esteem, and Confidence* (1994), maintained that a crisis exists in the way we educate our daughters, citing such revealing quotes as "Guys like it when you are helpless" (p. 21) and "Too cute to be competent" (p. 35). Orenstein worked with middle schools to examine female self-esteem and the differences between how boys and girls learn to think about themselves. Barrie Thorne's (1993) *Gender Play* takes a different approach, as it looks at both girls and boys. She maintained that gender cannot be examined in isolation, and looked at the why and how of gender separation and whether a culture of gender exists.

As Chapter 5 shows in greater detail, the American Association of University Women (AAUW) has been instrumental in bringing attention to the plight of girls in schools and in providing useful information. Several AAUW publications have done an excellent job in pointing out how schools often do not meet the needs of girls, and in describing programs and efforts that do work. *How Schools Shortchange Girls* (1992), for example, explains how girls experi-

> *Many educators need to change mindsets that favor boys and place girls in second-class positions.*

ence unequal educational experiences, and it also provides recommendations for educators and policymakers. Another AAUW publication, *Growing Smart: What's Working for Girls in School* (1995), reviews more than 500 studies and reports identifying themes and approaches that promote girls' achievement and healthy development.

A third AAUW publication, *Girls in the Middle: Working To Succeed in School* (1996), describes the challenges facing young adolescent females. One such challenge is that young adolescent girls learn the social patterns of the adult world at the same time they are actively interpreting the world and shaping their own values. They face a monumental task when confronted with this onslaught of cultural and personal messages about what it means to be female. The report goes on to describe what works for girls in middle schools and provides a new understanding of how schools use various education reforms to foster equitable environments for school achievement. The report calls for gender equity becoming a central aspect of school environments (just as we want for middle schools) and offers several directions to achieve that goal, such as committed adults taking risks and working to build coalitions and support networks, program development that makes gender issues visible in classrooms and schools, and policy initiatives to highlight the centrality of gender equity in the school mission.

How Schools Exacerbate Problems

It is fairly easy to identify what schools are now doing (and have done for decades) and what they need to do. Traditionally, schools have catered toward boys' academic achievement, self-esteem, and their perceptions of motivation, success, and individualism. The pendulum should not swing completely away from boys' perspectives—that would be as unfair as the situation now facing girls. To provide gender-equitable educational experiences, many educators need to change mindsets that favor boys and place girls in second-class positions. Changing personal and societal mindsets, however, cannot be done overnight—educators will need to work to recognize gender differences and to provide gender-responsive educational experiences. Only then will gender equity begin.

Teachers often base academic and social expectations on gender-specific mindsets, and provide educational experiences according to those expectations. Boys at the bottom of the class and boys at the top of the class attract a great deal of a teacher's attention. Teachers often hope their male prize pupils will become tomorrow's corporate presidents and civic leaders, and so they strive to reward them. Teachers fear that the boys at the bottom could become involved in serious trouble, and so they focus attention on controlling them. Both groups of boys are taught different lessons and socialized into distinct aspects of the male role in America. Whether viewed as being at the top or at the bottom, boys in general pay a significant price (Sadker & Sadker, 1994).

Similarly, and probably based on these gender-specific mindsets, teachers behave differently towards boys and girls. On the average, males tend to receive more criticism and suggestions for improvement, benefit from more frequent praise for correct answers, and have more contact with their teachers. Teachers tend to help boys more, encourage them more frequently, and, generally speaking, appear more concerned about their progress. Whether teachers think girls can "make it on their own," or they simply place less priority on girls' learning, evidence suggests that in regard to overall learning and academic achievement, teachers provide inequitable educational experiences. As an interesting note, the teachers' own sex did not affect these conclusions (Leder, 1992).

Educators' gender-specific mindsets often stem from societal and cultural attitudes toward gender. External and societal influences affect internal motivational beliefs and students' autonomous learning behaviors, and these in turn contribute to gender differences in achievement, especially mathematics achievement (Fennema & Peterson, 1985; Leder, 1992). Integral and interacting components of the model (Leder, 1992) include the cultural milieu; the behaviors, attitudes and expectations of socializers; the child's perceptions of these attitudes and expectations; the individual's goals and self-image; the perceptions of the value of the task; achievement behaviors; expectations; task-specific beliefs; past events as well as their interpretations; and the differential aptitudes of the child. The peer group and the media also act as important references for socialization and further perpetuate gender-role differentiation through gender-typed leisure activities, friendship patterns, subject preferences, and education and career intentions. Peer values reflect, reinforce, and shape differences in the beliefs, attitudes, and behaviors of the individuals who constitute the group (Leder, 1992). These peer values and influences might grow even more powerful when young adolescents perceive that teachers' and the overall school philosophies reflect gender-typed attitudes and activities.

Educators also exacerbate problems through their selection of textbooks and other curricular materials that are written primarily for males and from males' perspectives. The *Congressional Quarterly Researcher* ("Textbook Sexism," 1994) reported that most textbooks in the past, and some in the present, appear to be written from male perspectives. Specifically, males appear in more illustrations, more male contributions are described, and important women such as Catherine Littlefield Greene (who aided Eli Whitney with the invention of the cotton gin) are omitted.

Likewise, educators' selection of traditional teaching methods, curricular materials, and organizational patterns too often favor males' perspectives. Perhaps unconsciously, educators have provided educational experiences that cater toward male perspectives of thinking, perceiving, learning, and behaving. Clark (1994), in the "Education and Gender" issue of the *Congressional Quarterly Researcher*, reported that schools often employ teaching methods that do not reflect girls' learning styles. Clark maintained, for example, that schools usually cater toward the typical male preference for individualistic and competitive activities, rather than the cooperative activities often preferred by girls. Although Clark (1994) offered some interesting points, educators should remember that girls and boys should not be stereotypically portrayed as collaborators and competitors, respectively, and that these traits result more from socialization than from particular gender traits.

Developmental research, scholarly writings, and the popular press continue to enhance educators' awareness of how girls perceive learning and socialization. Individualism and competition have been mainstays of U.S. schools since their inception. Even today, some educators feel that individual work and group competition serve as motivators. Whether in spelling bees or a Jeopardy game, many schools teach competition and "rugged individualism." Educators now have sufficient evidence, however, to suggest that many girls learn better in situations where educators allow children to encourage, help, and assist one another.

Gender-Responsive Middle Schools

Young adolescents have gender differences (albeit most differences are socialized) that affect how they will learn, interact, and perceive all school experiences. In an effort to provide gender-equitable educational experiences, middle school educators must address those gender differences. Since developmental research and other informative publications offer insights into gender and its effects on education and learning, educators now can be sensitive to the differences and similarities in the genders. Gender-responsive educational experiences can become a reality in middle schools, if educators successfully tackle several challenges. When one considers the importance of young adolescents forming attitudes compatible with the ideals of a more egalitarian society, the need to meet the challenge of addressing gender differences becomes even more critical. What challenges face middle school educators as they work to provide gender-equitable educational experiences?

First, middle school educators should help both genders by taking an active stance against sexist and discriminatory practices, such as girls being discouraged from taking math, science, and technology classes. Because of young adolescents' previously mentioned developmental characteristics, educators in middle schools have an ideal opportunity to fight all forms of sexism and discrimination, to encourage girls to participate in math, science, and technology classes, and to teach both boys and girls to accept each other, regardless of gender.

Second, middle school educators should take deliberate professional action to provide gender-equitable middle schools. As Chapters 3 and 4 suggest in considerable detail, such professional action will include providing gender-fair curriculum, instructional approaches, and learning environments.

Third, middle school educators need to find additional sources of information on addressing gender differences (see Chapter 5). No longer can educators rely only on curricular, instructional, and learning environment resources that favor one perspective of learning. They need to gather the most reliable and useful resources available. Information on gender-equitable curriculum, instructional practices, and learning environments are available from state departments of education, organizations promoting equity and gender-fair schools, university resource centers, and professional associations.

Middle school educators' success in providing gender-responsive educational experiences will depend upon the extent of their efforts and their commitment. The benefits to young adolescents, their schools, their communities, and the nation itself will make the considerable effort worthwhile.

A National Middle School Association (NMSA) position paper, *This We Believe* (1995), describes responsive educational experiences for all young adolescents. Although *This We Believe* does not specifically call for gender-responsive educational experiences, it urges respect for diversity and a commitment to the ideals of a democratic society. Referring to positive school environments, for example, *This We Believe* states, "Students and adults recognize and accept one another's differences; and curiosity, creativity, and diversity are celebrated" (p. 19). The position taken on diversity in *This We Believe* can be construed to include recognition of and respect for gender diversity. The document calls for specific commitments, such as varied teaching and learning approaches, flexible organizational structures, positive school environments, high expectations for all students, and a challenging curriculum, whether traditional or integrated. Each of these commitments, as well as the overall theme and tone of *This We Believe*, can be considered a call to respect gender diversity and to develop educational experiences that reflect young adolescents' gender-specific needs.

Similarities of Goals of Middle Schools and Gender Equity

The middle school concept and the call for schools to recognize and respond to gender differences share several notable similarities. Both movements grew in popularity during the latter half of the 20th century and both reflect and complement each other in two distinct ways.

First, both share student-centered philosophies and actions—they both want to make schools more gender-equitable and reflective of student-centered philosophies and actions. The gender movement espouses the differences (and similarities) of both genders. Similarly, the middle school movement espouses a strong belief in helping, nurturing, promoting, and respecting individual learners. Both the gender equity and the middle school movements have a goal to recognize and respond to students' individual needs resulting from their gender differences, while respecting and noting similarities.

Second, both the gender equity and the middle school movements demonstrate the importance of respecting diversity in all its forms. Professionals calling for gender equity recognize the importance of differences and how they affect learning and socialization. Likewise, the middle school education movement espouses a genuine commitment to respecting, and responding to, young adolescents' diversity. For example, middle school perspectives espoused in *This We Believe* (NMSA, 1995) take the position that young adolescents' widely differing developmental characteristics should be reflected in teaching and learning experiences.

Third, both movements recognize how gender affects education and vice versa. We have already discussed books and periodicals that urge educators to recognize gender and the effects of gender on education. While only two of these publications (AAUW, 1996; Rothenberg, 1995) focus specifically on young adolescents and middle schools, they all have implications for middle school educators and an understanding of the early adolescence development period (what Brown and Gilligan [1992] called "the edge of adolescence" [p. 2]), which is the time when many girls begin to decline in self-esteem and achievement, and they begin to change their behaviors in order to be more "girl-like." While Myra Sadker started her efforts over 25 years ago with the book *Sexism in School and Society* (Frazier & Sadker, 1973), many excellent publications are relatively recent, published during the last decade or so. Again, one can conclude that while all levels of schooling need reforming, the early adolescence years are so instrumental in determining self-esteem, future academic achievement, and socialization that middle schools have a uniquely critical responsibility to address equitably the needs of both girls and boys.

Major Beliefs Underlying *Addressing Gender Differences in Young Adolescents*
Any discussion of the relationship among gender and socialization, self-esteem, academic achievement, lack of motivation to succeed, school participation, gender role attitudes and behaviors, and health concerns needs to be prefaced by a warning to consider the cultural, racial, socioeconomic, and individual differences of both boys and girls. Thornburg's (1982) assertion that diversity is the hallmark characteristic of young adolescents becomes even more important as one considers gender differences. Making generalizations about gender risks stereotyping and ignores individual differences. Educators have the professional responsibility to consider males and females as individuals, to consider each within their many cultures, and to avoid basing education decisions on stereotypes, false perceptions, and half-truths.

Several major beliefs underlie *Addressing Gender Differences in Young Adolescents*. These beliefs stem from the authors' research, firsthand experiences teaching female and male young adolescents, and a strong conviction that educational experiences at all levels, and especially the middle school, should be equitable for both girls and boys. Rather than being only lofty goals, gender-equitable middle school experiences can become a reality. Gender can be reflected in adviser-advisee and exploratory programs; the core, traditional, integrated, and exploratory curriculum; overall school environment; overall organizational and grouping patterns; and extracurricular activities. Research and writings provide a sufficient knowledge base that middle school educators can use to provide gender-responsive and gender-equitable educational experiences, instead of adhering to "a one-size-fits-all" policy for both genders.

The first belief holds that gender refers to both girls and boys. Both genders have their own unique differences, learning characteristics, and ways of thinking that are, in large part, a result of socialization and are not immutable. Boys and girls may negotiate developmental stages differently and experience different gender-specific issues, although socialization plays a significant role in the development of these differences and the perceptions of experiences. Middle level schools need to recognize and address both genders. One gender should neither be favored over the other one nor considered in gender-fixated perspectives.

Teachers, often unknowingly, perceive females and males from different perspectives. In one case, the parents of a 13-year-old girl attended a parent-teacher conference to learn what they could do to promote their daughter's progress in mathematics. The teacher actually downplayed the need for increased achievement and stated, "Your daughter is so beautiful—sometimes I just look at her during class and think what a beautiful girl she is." As the parents left the middle school, the father, who was concerned about the obvious downplaying of achievement and emphasis on beauty, asked the mother, "Do you think she would have made a similar comment about our son?" Both the mother and father thought the teacher's concern and comments would have been different if the conference had been about a son.

Rather than focusing attention toward only one gender, schools need to address the needs of both boys *and* girls, rather than catering to one gender at the expense of the other. For example, educators traditionally have adhered to curricular, organizational, and instructional practices that focus on boys' needs. Rather than totally reversing this tendency and focusing predominantly on girls, educators need to consider learning perspectives of *both* girls and boys and plan educational experiences for both. Rather than simply switching from one gender mindset to another, educators who consider gender perspectives will recognize the respective genders, and plan and teach accordingly.

Our second belief is that schools traditionally have catered to learning styles favored by many males. Educators, perhaps unknowingly, cater to boys' learning styles and perspectives toward motivation and success, and show more attention to males, especially high-achieving males. While males should neither be neglected nor overlooked, educational experiences also should be directed fairly and equitably toward girls. For example, middle school educators can allow, and in fact, encourage girls to work collaboratively in a competition-free environment.

The third belief underlying *Addressing Gender Differences in Young Adolescents* is that educators *can* provide gender-responsive educational experiences. To do so, they must recognize and understand girls' and boys' learning and developmental needs, make a commitment to provide fair and equitable experiences, and provide responsive curricular and instructional methods (e.g., cooperative learning), materials, and programs. For middle school educators, the challenge also includes learning how to most effectively use essential middle school concepts, such as adviser-advisee and exploratory programs.

Based upon these beliefs, we tried to reach several broad goals for *Addressing Gender Differences in Young Adolescents:*

Goal 1   Middle school educators should recognize gender differences among learners and realize how these differences affect learning, development, socialization, and perspectives toward motivation and competition.

Goal 2   Middle school educators should understand the research on gender, especially on topics such as how gender affects young adolescents' socialization, self-esteem, academic achievement, school participation, sex role attitudes and behaviors, health concerns, and moral development.

Goal 3   Middle school educators should understand how essential middle school concepts (such as adviser-advisee, exploratory programs, and a gender-responsive school environment, as well as the essentials described in *This We Believe* [National Middle School Association, 1995]) can be used to make middle schools more gender-equitable.

Goal 4   Middle school educators should understand how the middle school curriculum can reflect gender concerns; for example, through gender-responsive curricular materials, the integrated curriculum, and exploratory curriculum.

Goal 5   Middle school educators should understand where to locate additional information such as journal articles, books, state department publications, and professional association publications.

Summary

Middle school educators can make a significant contribution to young adolescents and society as a whole by providing gender-equitable educational experiences. While educational experiences reflecting gender can benefit learners at all developmental periods, several developmental characteristics suggest that the early adolescence period is an optimal time to provide such experiences. Learners in the childhood developmental stage might be too young or too dependent on their parents' beliefs, and older students may have already formed undesirable attitudes. A call is being issued to recognize early adolescence as an ideal time to recognize gender differences and to instill respect for one another.

References

American Association of University Women. (1992). *How schools shortchange girls.* Annapolis Junction, MD: Author.

American Association of University Women. (1995). *Growing smart: What's working for girls in school.* Annapolis Junction, MD: Author.

American Association of University Women. (1996). *Girls in the middle: Working to succeed in school.* Annapolis Junction, MD: Author.

Brown, L. M., & Gilligan, C. (1992). *Meeting at the crossroads: Women's psychology and girls' development.* Cambridge, MA: Harvard.

Clark, C. S. (1994). Education and gender: The issues. *Congressional Quarterly Researcher, 4*(21), 483-487, 490-491.

Education and gender. (1994). *Congressional Quarterly Researcher, 4*(21), 481-504.

Fennema, E., & Peterson, P. L. (1985). Autonomous learning behavior: A possible explanation of gender-related differences in mathematics. In L. C. Wilkinson & C. B. Marrett (Eds.), *Gender-related differences in classroom interactions* (pp. 17-35). New York: Academic Press.

Frazier, N., & Sadker, M. (1973). *Sexism in school and society.* New York: Harper & Row.

Leder, G. C. (1992). Mathematics and gender: Changing perspectives. In D. Grouws (Ed.), *Handbook of research on mathematics teaching and learning* (pp. 597-622). New York: Macmillan.

Manning, M. L. (1993). *Developmentally appropriate middle level schools.* Olney, MD: Association for Childhood Education International.

Manning, M. L. (1994). *Celebrating diversity: Multicultural education in middle level schools.* Columbus, OH: National Middle School Association.

National Middle School Association. (1995). *This we believe: Developmentally responsive middle level schools.* Columbus, OH: Author.

Orenstein, P. (1994). *SchoolGirls: Young women, self-esteem, and the confidence gap.* New York: Doubleday and American Association of University Women.

Pipher, M. (1994). *Reviving Ophelia: Saving the lives of adolescent girls.* New York: Grosset/Putnam.

Rothenberg, D. (1995, September). Supporting girls in early adolescence. *ERIC Digest,* 1-2.

Sadker, M., & Sadker, D. (1994). *Failing at fairness: How America's schools cheat girls.* New York: Scribner.

Textbook sexism. (1994). *Congressional Quarterly Researcher, 4*(21), 496.

Thornburg, H. (1982). The total early adolescent in contemporary society. *High School Journal, 65,* 272-278.

Thorne, B. (1993). *Gender play: Girls and boys in school.* New Brunswick, NJ: Rutgers.

Women's Educational Equity Act. (1997). http: www.edc.org/Women's equity.

Chapter 2

Gender Differences in Young Adolescents: Research and Literature

*S*uzy is a 14-year-old female in the 8th grade (preparing for high school) who lives with her two-parent, college-educated family in the middle-class suburbs of a large city. While Suzy has above-average intelligence, she makes below-average grades and lacks motivation. She does not participate in extracurricular activities, but she has tried out for a school play and for the cheerleading team.

Suzy has many close friends, both females and males; however, most are female. Females will visit to spend the night, and males occasionally visit in the afternoon after school. Her one or two best and closest friends appear to be her highest priority—she socializes in school at every opportunity.

When she has a choice in what courses to take, she avoids mathematics and sciences and chooses those that allow her to read. The same is true with her middle school exploratories. She elected more music and art courses. Unfortunately, her teachers and guidance counselor have not encouraged her to take mathematics and science courses other than those required. She says she does not like mathematics and science; she might be one or more grade levels behind by now.

Suzy is an attractive and healthy young adolescent. She does not have a weight problem or any skin problems. She says little about her appearance. She does not appear to have any health problems or concerns. Neither is there any evidence of alcohol, drug, or tobacco use.

From a moral development perspective, she sometimes has difficulty telling the truth and shows few signs of guilt (albeit appearances can be deceiving). As far as her parents and teachers know, her "untruths" have been about homework and grades. Suzy refuses to meet with her guidance counselor, because "there is nothing wrong," and only talks to the teachers she likes.

She usually waits for males to take the lead and to show her how something is done. While her mother and father would like for her to be more assertive and take a lead, she prefers to just follow others. Suzy does not mind (and, in fact, seems to prefer) when males take the lead in activities.

Her parents have met with the teachers and guidance counselor on many oc casions, but see little progress. Her teachers like her, encourage her, and offer their help, but she shows little inclination to take advantage of their offers. Her teachers and parents feel that she can make average or perhaps above-average grades, but Suzy is satisfied with "Ds" or "Cs." She appears to experience no embarrassment or shame associated with her lack of academic achievement. Her parents have worked to help her and have addressed her lack of academic achievement since the 3rd grade, but they have "come up short." Suzy has a mind of her own and seems content with her academic performance and lack of participation in extracurricular activities.

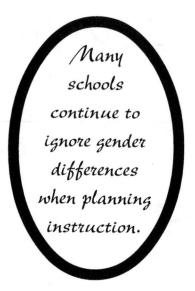

Many schools continue to ignore gender differences when planning instruction.

Overview

While Suzy's story sounds stereotypical and contrived, it is unfortunately true—except for her name (which the authors have changed). All too often, girls (and boys) do not take full advantage of the opportunities provided by middle schools. Girls often have one or two close friends who take precedence over academic and overall school success, they enroll in mathematics and science courses in disproportionately low numbers, they do not see a need to seek the guidance counselor's help, and they often wait for (or feel coerced to wait for) boys to take the lead. Middle school educators and guidance counselors need to understand gender differences and how both genders are socialized from early childhood to think and act from gender-specific perspectives.

As we indicated in Chapter 1, the challenge for the 21st century will be to recognize gender differences in young adolescents and plan gender-responsive educational experiences—the topics of Chapters 3 and 4. Research increasingly describes the differences (e.g., socialization, self-esteem, achievement, motivation and school participation) between females and males. As suggested in Chapter 1, however, educators need to remember that many gender differences might actually result from girls and boys being socialized or conditioned to adopt gender-specific behaviors and ways of thinking, learning, and behaving. In fact, research has improved in both quantity and quality to a point where middle school educators can now identify specific gender differences (Manning, 1993a, 1993b; Manning & Hager, 1995) and provide educational experiences and classroom environments that reflect a recognition and understanding of those differences (Butler & Sperry, 1991; Manning & Hager, 1995). While we will examine gender differences for both females and males, we will focus on females' gender differences in this chapter because schools traditionally have based educational experiences on methods to which many males respond well.

A Clarion Call to Action

Research and scholarly writings on gender differences have issued a clarion call for middle school educators, guidance counselors, and other professionals to take definitive action to ensure that educational experiences reflect both females' and males' gender-specific characteristics. While research on gender differences provides directions for educators planning and implementing educational experiences, the fact remains that many schools continue to ignore gender differences when planning instructional experiences and educational environments. Educators have not heeded, to any significant extent, research and scholarly writing indicating that schools:

- focus toward male perspectives, thus possibly placing females at risk (Shakeshaft, 1986)
- allow males to dominate classroom activities
- provide curricular materials focusing primarily on male accomplishments and male figures
- allow females to experience various inequities in schools (AAUW, 1992; "Education and Gender," 1994; "Girls Can't Escape Sexism," 1994).

Traditionally, educators of all levels, including middle school educators, have geared teaching-learning experiences toward males (Butler & Sperry, 1991). By focusing more attention on boys or failing to understand gender differences, Suzy's middle school may have failed to recognize how Suzy's and other girls' problems were related to gender. Rather than continuing such practices during these particularly impressionable developmental years, middle school educators should take a strong stand toward providing gender equitable instruction for both females and males. Likewise, counselors need to guide both girls and boys into subjects and courses without regard to gender-specific mindsets. Only then will girls like Suzy have an equal opportunity to achieve academically and to have equal access to all school activities.

Gender Differences

The terms "sex" and "gender" are used inconsistently in the literature. Increasingly, "sex difference" is used to refer to biological differences between females and males, and "gender differences" to refer to nonbiological characteristics, psychological features, and social categories (Leder, 1992, p. 600).

In the remainder of this chapter, we direct attention to the research on gender and social networks and socialization, gender role attitudes and behaviors, self-esteem, moral development and reasoning, health concerns, academic achievement, and school participation. We want to keep Suzy in mind as we consider the research findings; we also want to begin to think about how middle school educators can address Suzy's gender differences and those of other girls like her (the topics of Chapter 3 and Chapter 4). Whenever possible, research will focus specifically on gender differences in young adolescents and on *both* boys and girls. When it becomes necessary to use research from other age groups, the relevant age or grade level will be given.

Socialization, Friendships, and Interpersonal Relationships

Socialization and friendship development are important to young adolescents, both girls and boys. Middle school educators detect differences, however, in the way the two genders socialize, and in the way they form and maintain friendships. The importance of socialization and friendship formation during early adolescence has been documented sufficiently (Crockett, Losoff, & Petersen, 1984; DuBois & Hirsch, 1993; Manning & Allen, 1987). Unfortunately, fewer studies have focused specifically on 10- to 14-year-old females' friendship patterns and peer relationships. Since crucial friendship formation occurs during the 10- to 14-year-old age period, gender differences in social networks and peer relations deserve to be understood and addressed.

Middle school educators can attest to the fact that young adolescents place considerable priority on friendships and socialization (just as Suzy considered her friends more important than her academic achievement). Examining the role of gender in young adolescents' socialization, Benenson (1990) studied both females and males to determine their social networks. The subjects rated best friends, measured peer group acceptance, and described each same-sex child in the class. Benenson concluded that attributes considered important in themselves and their same-sex friends differed according to gender; and that males had larger social networks or number of friends than females. Also, males exhibited more agreement than females in the attributes used to describe same-sex peers. Males showed greater concern with attributes considered to be important for status in the peer group, while females demonstrated concern with attributes necessary for relationships with a few friends (Benenson, 1990). Suzy's friendships (i.e., the relationships she had with her one or two best and closest friends) reflect Benenson's research conclusions.

How do middle school girls and boys differ in their willingness to ask peers for help? To what extent do young adolescents want to be considered part of a group? Downe and McDougall (1995) studied gender differences among 6th-graders, levels of attraction to and perceived acceptance of peers, and students' willingness to seek assistance from peers. Specifically, they sought to determine how females' and males' levels of attraction to the peer group and perceived acceptance by the peer group affected their tendencies to seek help in solving problems.

They found that females showed significantly greater willingness than males to receive help with a decision about a school play; children of both sexes preferred older, same-sex helpers; males demonstrated greater willingness to receive help from an older male; and females showed more willingness to receive help from an older female. Overall, children's perceptions of acceptance by the classroom peer group and their attraction to the peer group did not have a significant influence on either their willingness to receive help or their helper preference. Downe's and McDougall's (1995) research on the interpersonal dynamics of females and males can be particularly helpful to middle school educators as they plan opportunities for young adolescents to work in small groups, engage in peer-tutoring, or participate in cooperative learning groups.

Gender role attitudes, orientations, and behaviors are other important topics for middle school educators to understand. Many variables—individuality, family, culture, and socioeconomic level—will affect young adolescent girls' and boys' attitudes and behaviors. Therefore, while it is worthwhile to be familiar with selected research, it will always be necessary to learn about specific individuals.

In their study of differences in gender role attitudes and actual behavior, Nelson and Keith (1990) interviewed girls and boys in grades 5 through 8 and sought to determine female and male gender role attitude and behavior development. The findings differed between young adolescents' attitudes and actual behavior. While both males and females demonstrated highly nontraditional sex role attitudes, for example, females proved significantly more nontraditional in their gender role behaviors. Both genders demonstrated more nontraditionalism in role attitudes than in actual role behaviors.

Other research findings (Nelson & Keith, 1990) show how the level of traditionalism in females' gender role attitude development is significantly influenced by maternal employment, the level of traditionalism in the father's gender role attitudes, the amount of time the father spent with the daughter, and the father's chronological age. In contrast, the mother's level of traditionalism influenced males' gender role attitude development, the degree of closeness to the mother reported by the son, and both the mother's and the father's perception of pubertal age. Nelson and Keith emphasized the complexity of young adolescents' gender role attitude development and considered gender role attitude and actual behavior to be separate and distinct processes.

Boys also are socialized by parents and other significant adults to adopt specific gender role attitudes and actual behaviors. While girls learn early to cooperate and compromise, boys learn that the rough world requires competition and individualism (Sadker & Sadker, 1994). As Sadker and Sadker (1994) wrote, boys are encouraged to "be cool, [not] show emotion, repress feelings, be aggressive, compete, and win" (p. 220). Girls typically learn to be nurturers, and boys learn that showing emotions toward others should not receive high priority. Males who have opportunities to care for younger brothers and sisters, however, become less aggressive and more nurturing in their relationships. While parents encourage empathy in daughters, caring boys may be seen as too gentle. In essence, both girls and boys are socialized to adopt gender-specific role attitudes and actual behaviors. Both males and females clearly benefit from the experience of caring for others, and if these opportunities are denied, boys may lose touch with their own emotions (Sadker & Sadker, 1994).

Sadker and Sadker (1994) report the results of a study that showed how boys often try to hide emotions. When researchers asked girls and boys to recall whether they felt afraid, sad, disgusted, or guilty in the last month, males denied experiencing these feelings. When researchers asked boys to keep diaries of their feelings, however, all these feelings surfaced. Through their socialization to think and act in accordance with a specific gender role, boys often deny their feelings (Sadker & Sadker, 1994).

Self-Esteem

Was self-esteem the reason why Suzy underachieved academically, waited for boys to take the lead, elected not to participate in extracurricular activities, and opted out of taking additional mathematics and science courses? Research is fairly conclusive that both girls and boys, especially girls, experience declines in self-esteem during the middle school years (Brown & Gilligan, 1990; "Education and Gender," 1994; Jackson, Hodge, & Ingram, 1994; Loeb & Horst, 1978; Lundeberg, Fox, & Puncochar, 1994; Robison-Awana, Kehle, & Jenson, 1986; Schmuck & Schmuck, 1994).

Middle school educators long have recognized the importance of positive self-esteem on young adolescents' academic achievement, socialization, and long-term goals. As discussed in Chapters 3 and 4, educators undoubtedly can address these topics through gender-equitable exploratory and advisory programs, as well as through gender-fair school environments. Research on gender and self-esteem indicates that this important dimension, which declines in females as they grow older, includes aspects such as stereotyping, self-ratings, efforts to boost self-esteem, effects on body image, and effects on academic achievement. Suzy's problems, like those of many other girls her age, could have been a result of declining self-esteem. We offer ways to improve self-esteem in girls and boys in Chapter 3 and Chapter 4.

Most middle school educators realize that self-esteem probably affects all aspects of young adolescents' personal lives, including academic achievement. The effects of self-esteem on young adolescent females' academic achievement, overall motivation, and general outlook on life should alert perceptive middle school educators to the need for gender-equitable school experiences designed to increase females' self-esteem.

Gilligan and her colleagues (Brown & Gilligan, 1990) found that girls' levels of self-confidence remain fairly high until age 11 or 12. Until then, they tend to be quite perceptive about relationship issues and assertive about their feelings. Around adolescence, however, they accept stereotyped notions of how they should be, and they repress their true feelings for more traditionally accepted ones. Both girls and boys often are socialized by educators, parents, and the greater community to think and behave in gender-specific ways.

As females recognize that they are not being themselves, their self-confidence falters. Only those who continue to be honest with themselves and with others—by acknowledging their true feelings and expressing them appropriately—are able to stay in healthy relationships with themselves, with others, and with the adult society they are entering. These girls' self-esteem stays high, they see themselves as competent, and they often choose more nontraditional careers (Brown & Gilligan, 1990). A broad-based survey sponsored by the American Association of University Women (AAUW) of 3,000 children in grades 4 through 10 yielded similar results (Daley, 1991). Although boys' self-worth also dropped by high school age, they were still ahead of the girls and their drop was less.

The AAUW survey also found culture to be a factor in self-esteem. Many more African American girls were still confident in high school compared to European and Hispanic girls, and European girls lost their self-assurance the earliest of all three groups. African American girls may feel more self-confident because they often see strong women around them. They seem less dependent on school achievement for their self-esteem, drawing their sense of themselves more from family and community (Daley, 1991).

Lundeberg, Fox, and Puncochar (1994) reported less self-esteem in females as early as the 6th grade, with these differences increasing with age. Females in elementary, middle, and secondary schools experience continuous decreases in self-esteem of 60 percent, 37 percent, and 29 percent, respectively ("Education and Gender," 1994). This lack of confidence, however, often does not result from a corresponding lack of ability. Instead, even when females achieve as well or better than their male counterparts, they tend to underestimate their ability and to overestimate others' abilities (Lundeberg, Fox, & Puncochar, 1994).

Jackson, Hodge, and Ingram (1994) have reported a relationship between self-esteem and gender stereotyping that could have contributed to Suzy's problems. As Suzy's self-esteem dipped, she could have felt the need to conform to gender expectations generally approved by society as a whole. Specifically, self-esteem scores usually correlate with stereotypes (i.e., both genders tend to score higher on self-esteem dimensions that stereotypically reflect their gender). Likewise, females and males draw from different domains of self-perceived strength in determining their self-esteem. For example, females develop their self-esteem based on relationships with others (i.e., a sense of connectedness) while males develop their self-esteem from separation from others (i.e., a sense of independence).

What do young adolescents use as a basis for determining their self-esteem? How do the different genders try to improve self-esteem? In their study of gender differences in young adolescents, Loeb and Horst (1978) concluded that males rate themselves higher in self-esteem than females do. They also found, however, that girls and boys tried to boost self-esteem in different ways. Males who lacked positive self-esteem used other sources, such as academic achievement, to boost their self-esteem. Females, on the other hand, often did not consider academic achievement to be a boost to self-esteem, despite the fact that females generally receive higher grades from their teachers.

Boys pay a significant toll in their attempts to boost self-esteem. Sadker and Sadker reported on a study that asked boys (in this case, high school boys) how they wanted to remembered. The options included "most popular," "athletic star," or "brilliant student." Forty-four percent of the teenage boys selected the option "athletic star." When asked who they would prefer as a friend, 56 percent of the boys selected an "athlete but not a scholar," while "scholar but not an athlete" was chosen by less than 20 percent (Sadker & Sadker, 1994). In fact, succeeding at a sport has the potential for increasing self-esteem by bringing rewards, developing leadership ability and a sense of teamwork, and offering the satisfaction gained from playing well (Sadker & Sadker, 1994). Although this study focused on high school boys, middle school boys also experience problems with self-esteem and often try athletics as a means of enhancing these feelings. Unfortunately, boys seeking to raise their self-esteem through athletics experience considerable pain and suffering. They are subject to being cut from the team and ridiculed by more able athletes. Furthermore, aggression, kept to a minimum in the classroom, is often encouraged by coaches.

While observers of young adolescents long have thought that rapidly changing physical development had corresponding effects on psychosocial development, one study documented a significant relationship between gender differences, self-concept, and body image. One generalization about gender differences is that males feel more positively about and are more satisfied with their bodies than females. Females, on the other hand, assign more discriminating and different values to different aspects of their bodies. Changes affecting the female body have the potential for making girls disappointed in their bodies, while the male may be more concerned with task mastery and effectiveness than with physical appearance (Koff, Rierdan, & Stubbs, 1990).

According to developmental research, the relationship between school achievement and psychological adjustment differs for males and females during early adolescence. Roberts, Sarigiani, Petersen, and Newman (1990) examined how gender differences affect the relationship between school achievement and self-image. Their study showed this relationship to be more positive for males than for females. Likewise, the relationship between achievement and self-image decreased for females and increased for males during the transition into adolescence. Specifically, the relationship between achievement and self-image for 6th-grade males increased during the transition and remained stable as they moved into the 8th grade, yet the relationship decreased for females during this same period.

A number of studies have focused on self-esteem and academic achievement, while other studies have dealt only with academic achievement among females. Remember Suzy's reluctance to participate in mathematics and science subjects—she felt uncomfortable in these areas or perhaps did not feel capable of competing with the boys. Research indicates that gender differences generally begin to surface during the middle school grades. Few consistent differences in mathematics performance manifest themselves at the early primary school level. In fact, few gender differences in average mathematics proficiency exist before age 9. Gender differences begin to occur at age 13 and increase substantially by age 17, especially at the upper proficiency levels (Kahle & Meece, 1994). Whether or not gender differences are found seems to depend on the content and format of the test administered, the age level at which testing takes place, and whether classroom grades or standardized tests of achievement are

> *Gender differences begin to occur at age 13 and increase substantially by age 17.*

used (Leder, 1992). Other barriers to females achieving in mathematics might be high mathematics anxiety, low parental expectations, and competitive classroom climates (Kahle & Meece, 1994).

Roberts and Petersen (1992) studied 242 young adolescents over a three-year period to determine the relationship between self-image and academic achievement in mathematics and science, as measured by grade averages. As might be expected, both males and females with higher mathematics and science grade point averages demonstrated higher self-image scores. Females with As in mathematics showed almost no change in self-image from 7th to the 8th grade. Disturbingly, females with mathematics grade point averages of D or lower showed decreases in self-image from 7th to 8th grade (Roberts & Petersen, 1992).

Fortunately, there is progress to note. Several studies (AAUW, 1992; Hyde, Fennema, & Lamon, 1990; Linn & Hyde, 1989) point to a decrease in the gender gap in mathematics achievement. An analysis of the research on mathematics and science achievement reveals an interesting finding: The gender gap is closing in mathematics achievement, especially during the middle school years (Kahle & Meece, 1994). Gender differences in mathematics achievement do not occur with any consistency until the late high school years, when girls begin to take fewer mathematics courses than boys (Kahle & Meece, 1994). When girls enroll in the same number and kinds of mathematics courses that boys do, gender differences in test scores, although not eliminated, decline (Kahle & Meece, 1994).

Fennema and Peterson (1985) found that time spent on competitive mathematics activities was significantly related to boys', but not girls', achievement in mathematics. For girls, mathematics achievement appeared to be enhanced more by participation in cooperative activities (Leder, 1992).

The gap in science achievement increases from age 9 to 13, although most boys and girls enroll in similar courses during those years. Several different sources of gender differences in science participation and achievement, ranging from cognitive abilities to sociocultural stereotyping of science as a masculine pursuit, have been studied. Researchers who have gone into science classrooms to delineate differential participation patterns have found that girls do not have equal opportunities to learn science (Kahle & Meece, 1994), which is yet another reason why Suzy may be reluctant to learn more about science.

Moral Development and Reasoning

In their study of specific incidents evoking guilt, Williams and Bybee (1994) studied gender differences in 5th-, 8th-, and 11th-graders. The number of students experiencing guilt from a neglect of responsibilities or a failure to attain ideals increases with grade levels. William and Bybee reached the following conclusions: parents evoke guilt in the highest percentage of students at all grade levels; and a greater percentage of male than female participants report guilt over property damage, fighting, and victimization of animals, as well as from events involving casual acquaintances and adults who may be victims of such actions. Guilt over events such as inner thoughts, however, is no more prevalent among female than male subjects.

A greater percentage of females than males reported guilt over incidents that violate norms of compassion and interpersonal trust (e.g., inconsiderateness and lying) and that involve intimate others (e.g., parents and extended family)—very similar to the kinds of untruths told by Suzy. Females are not more likely than males to mention guilt involving siblings and friends, perhaps because age-mates are victims of aggressive as well as inconsiderate behaviors. Research findings do not support the view that males are more likely than females to report guilt over clear-cut violations of rules and regulations, such as disobedience, stealing, and truancy (Williams & Bybee, 1994).

Morality has at least two major dimensions: justice with regard to individual rights, and care elicited by a sense of responsibility in relationships. Gilligan has developed a different way of looking at morality, one that seems to fit in more with a female viewpoint (Gilligan, 1982). As suggested in Chapter 3, morality, and females' and males' different ways of looking at morality, can be explored in both advisory sessions and exploratory programs.

Gilligan (1982) pointed out that male and female beliefs about the nature of reality differ significantly. Before Gilligan's work, research and thinking about moral development tended only to reflect male perspectives. Gilligan noted that males' and females' differing patterns of psychosocial development result in varying patterns of thinking.

In an example from early adolescence, Gilligan compared the cases of Jake and Amy, two 11-year-olds. Upon asking each youngster the question "When responsibility to oneself and responsibility to others conflict, how should one choose?" Gilligan (1982) received the following responses:

Jake: You go about one-fourths to others and three-fourths to yourself.

Amy: Well, it really depends on the situation. If you have a responsibility with someone else, then you should keep it to a certain extent, but to the extent that it is really going to hurt you or stop you from doing something that you really want, then I think maybe you should put yourself first. But if it is your responsibility to somebody really close to you, you've just got to decide in that situation which is more important, yourself or that person, and like I said, it really depends on what kind of person you are and how you feel about the other persons involved. (pp. 35-36)

Although Jake's and Amy's answers seem stereotypically male and female, these general points should be kept in mind:

- Women tend to have different ways of thinking about the world than men.
- In many cases the direct, straightforward approach of the male model may be insensitive to others.
- When viewed from an alternative perspective, the female model may be more conceptually advanced.

From three studies of individuals interviewed about moral conflicts and choices, Gilligan derived her own theory: Men reason morally through a voice of individual rights and justice, but a different voice, one of connection and caring, belongs primarily to women.

Recent research seems to bear out this dichotomy and to suggest that it first shows up in early adolescence (Skoe & Gooden, 1993). Forty-six 11- and 12-year-olds, both girls and boys, were interviewed using the ethic-of-care technique. These interviews incorporate one real-life conflict, along with three hypothetical dilemmas involving family and friends. One question, for example, asked what a hypothetical young person should do if "Nicole" or "Jason" has accepted a friend's dinner invitation and then receives an invitation to see a favorite rock band on the same evening.

When scored according to ethic-of-care levels, girls scored higher than boys. The girls generated more personal real-life dilemmas (those involving a specific person or group of people whom the subject knows well), whereas the boys were more likely to talk about moral conflicts involving people they did not know well, institutions, or issues intrinsic to the self. Girls also tended to be more concerned than boys about maintaining friendships and not hurting other people. The boys were more likely to be concerned about themselves, emphasizing, for example, the need to stay out of trouble (Skoe & Gooden, 1993).

Looking at the effects of gender on moral development of Hawaiian youths, Daniels, D'Andrea, and Heck (1995) studied children and adolescents from the

5th, 7th, 9th, and 11th grades. Their study sought to determine whether Carol Gilligan's theories (Gilligan, 1979, 1982) of content and process of moral development among females held true among persons of differing cultures. Using fables to study moral development, they asked participants to offer a reaction ("care," "justice," and some combination thereof) to a dilemma. They found no gender differences in moral reasoning between female and male Hawaiian youths. In addition, a "care" perspective dominated the responses offered by both male and females.

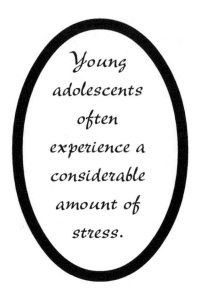

Young adolescents often experience a considerable amount of stress.

Health Concerns

Studies on health concerns of male and female young adolescents have focused on topics such as illness behaviors, depressive symptoms, alcohol and substance use, eating disorders, and stress. The selection of these topics and studies neither negates other health concerns among young adolescents nor downplays any special concerns of females.

In an examination of gender differences in young adolescents' self-assessed health status and illness behaviors, Alexander (1989) studied 8th-graders. Identified gender differences included young adolescent males and females using different "yardsticks" (p. 475) for judging health status. Females, who already had undergone most of their physical changes, associated emotional and social concerns with poorer perceived health, while males associated physical concerns with fair or poor health. Furthermore, females attended school more often when ill, yet missed more days from school due to emotional concerns.

Baron and Campbell (1993) studied 153 French Canadian middle adolescents to determine gender differences in depressive symptoms. They found that depressive symptoms are more characteristic of females. Adolescent females, in general, report more depressive symptoms, some of which represent stereotypically feminine characteristics such as weight loss, loss of appetite, and crying (Baron & Campbell, 1993). The researchers also found that, in general, females are more prone to exhibit expressive symptoms, but when overall depression scores are high, both males and females express symptoms characteristic of their socially prescribed gender roles. Males, for example, exhibit work inhibition and somatic symptoms.

Examining substance use, gender, and grade level, Nagel, McDougall, and Granby (1996) surveyed 4th-, 6th-, 8th-, and 10th-graders for alcohol and substance use. In keeping with the focus of this publication, we will report the research findings for grades 6 and 8 only. A multiplicity of social, economic, cultural and demographic variables should be considered when analyzing the use of alcohol and other drugs. As probably expected, substance use increases with grade levels. While relatively small increases exist between grades 6 and 8, significant increases occur between grades 4, 8, and 10. The following gender differences can be found: 1) females report higher usage than males for over-the-counter drugs, 2) males and females report about the same use of wine, and 3) males report higher usage of beer, smoking tobacco, hard liquor, and chewing tobacco. Also, males reported a slightly greater use of the other listed drugs. Still, in most cases, only slight gender differences can be found in the usage of alcohol and other drugs.

Many males face significant risks associated with alcohol and substance use. Boys are three times more likely to become alcohol dependent and 50 percent more likely to use illicit drugs. Men account for more than 90 percent of alcohol- and drug-related arrests. Many of these problems could have originated from problems experienced in school. Risk-taking behavior extends beyond alcohol and substance use. The leading cause of death among young boys is accidents, and teenage boys are more likely to die from gunshot wounds than from all natural causes combined (Sadker & Sadker, 1994).

Another health concern, eating disorders, should be cause for alarm for middle school educators, especially since early adolescence might be a developmental stage when females and males run the risk of developing anorexia nervosa or bulimia. Felker and Stivers (1994) studied the relationship of gender to the risk of these eating disorders. While females run the greater risk of being anorexic, males also developed anorexia nervosa (females: 95 percent; males: 5 percent). While 32.1 percent of the females were at risk of developing an eating disorder, only 22.8 percent of the males were (Felker & Stivers, 1994).

As middle school educators realize, young adolescents often experience a considerable amount of stress. Goodman, Brumley, Schwartz, and Purcell (1993) examined the relationship of gender and negative stress in 5th- and 6th-graders' school adjustment. In their research review, they reported considerable disagreement regarding whether males or females experience the most negative stress. Males experienced more stress than females and demonstrated more maladjusted behaviors, yet they did not engage in more acting out (however, the study suggested caution with this conclusion because teachers might use different "acting out" [p. 340] standards for females and males). Also, they suggest that gender might be a more central factor than development in school adjustment and stress. Sadker and Sadker (1994) also suggest that males as well as females are victims of stress and its consequences. In fact, boys are nine times as likely to suffer from hyperactivity and higher levels of academic stress.

Academic Achievement
The literature on gender differences and academic achievement makes engaging reading for middle school educators. The research on female adolescent devel-

opment has revealed several interesting findings concerning course selection and actual achievement levels. In general, this research has taken three directions: general academic achievement, academic achievement in mathematics, and academic achievement in science. The previous section on academic achievement looked only at its relationship to self-esteem; in this section, however, we look only at academic achievement in general.

Studying both middle and high school students, Williams (1994) studied gender differences in students' judgments concerning their ability to meet successful levels of performance and their actual performance levels in mathematics, reading, English, and science. Approximately equal numbers of male and female students overestimated their performance capabilities. Findings showed that students with higher expectations for success generally had higher performance outcome scores, and the relationships between judgments for performance and actual performance proved stronger in mathematics than in other subject areas.

Investigating gender, African American culture, and academic achievement, Pollard (1993) found high achieving students (both middle and high school) demonstrated more positive self-perceptions, more interpersonal support, and more active problem-solving. Also, female students had the highest academic achievement. Pollard also found that African American students reported gaining interpersonal support from outside the school, rather than from within, because schools often fail to provide the resources and support that they need. Another finding suggested that males feel they receive less academic support from teachers than females do.

Examining perceived opportunities, Danziger (1983) proposed gender-related differences in perceived opportunities, which subsequently affected education aspirations. For example, males' academic ability and achievement strongly influenced their perceptions of education possibilities, yet social factors had greater effects on females' aspirations.

While females achieve higher overall grades prior to the middle school, many males also experience continued academic difficulties in school. From elementary school through high school, for example, boys receive lower report card grades; by middle school, they are far more likely to be grade repeaters and school dropouts. Similarly, boys make up the majority of the students identified for special education programs. They represent 58 percent of those in classes for the mentally retarded, and 80 percent of those in classes for the emotionally disturbed. Many teachers encourage boys to pursue unrealistically high career goals, thus resulting in boys feeling like failures and experiencing a prolonged sense of frustration (Sadker & Sadker, 1994).

Looking specifically at mathematics achievement and grades, females throughout most school years demonstrate higher overall academic achievement than males do. Prior to the middle grades, females score as well in mathematics as males (Petersen & Wittig, 1979). Terwilliger and Titus (1995) studied participants in the University of Minnesota Talented Youth Mathematics Program (UMTYMP) to determine gender differences of mathematically talented youth on a variety of attitudinal measures related to academic success. Specific items examined included interest, motivation, confidence, readiness, support, priorities, and stereotypes. Males showed significantly higher levels of motivation, confidence, and interest in mathematics than females. Despite efforts of the UMTYMP program staff to provide an atmosphere that supported and encouraged females, gender differences increased over the two years. In fact, Terwilliger and Titus found that females' enthusiasm waned over the two years. Peer pressure and the competition of emerging extracurricular and social interests may partially account for the decline. As we show in Chapters 3 and 4, middle school educators can use many strategies to avoid the pitfalls of competition and individualism.

Ramos and Lambating (1996) looked at achievement in terms of risk taking and its relation to mathematics success, and examined whether females were reluctant risk takers. They began by saying that students more prone to taking risks perform better on mathematics tests and that males tend to be greater risk takers. This might explain males' better performance on mathematics achievement. While admitting that all research does not support their theory, Ramos and Lambating (1996) documented research showing females' reluctance to guess on multiple choice tests and tendency to omit more questions regardless of type (e.g., true-false, multiple choice, and relationship analysis). They recommend that educators constantly assure females of their ability and competence in mathematics and that test constructors consider the effects that their directions on guessing may have on test takers, especially females. Others suggest that when educators reword higher level mathematics to fit female perspectives, females show as much capability at mathematical analysis as males do (Berkovitz, 1979; Butler & Sperry, 1991).

Jeffe (1995) studied the historical nature of females' difficulties in science, and found that the historical, social, and political context of women's experiences in science challenges the stereotype that females "historically" (p. 206) have had a difficult time in science. Attempting to debunk this stereotype, she explained that ancient biographies of many women indicate an interest in science, contrary to the belief that women historically were not interested in science. Jeffe also explored the "weaker sex" (p. 210) argument, the idea of women being more suited for domesticity than other occupational opportunities. Again, Jeffe looked at gender and achievement, especially in regards to science, in a new light, and maintained that many common beliefs are only stereotypes that have been perpetuated throughout history.

Judith Meech and Jacquelynne Jones (1996) looked at motivation and strategy use and questioned whether females were rote learners. Meech and Jones (1996) looked at 5th- and 6th-grade students' self-reports of confidence, motivational goals, and learning strategies. Overall, they found few gender differences. Compared with females, males showed greater confidence in their science abilities;

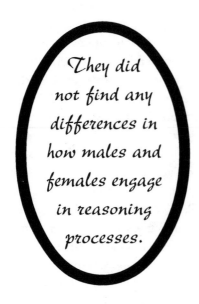

They did not find any differences in how males and females engage in reasoning processes.

average-achieving females reported greater use of meaningful learning strategies, whereas low-ability males reported a stronger mastery orientation than low-ability females; and both genders showed greater confidence and mastery motivation in small-group than in whole-class instruction. There was no evidence that females are more likely to learn science in a rote or verbatim manner than males (Meech & Jones, 1996). Along the same line of thinking, Valanides (1996) worked with 7th-, 8th, and 9th-grade students to determine their reasoning modes. Valanides did not find any gender differences in how males and females engage in reasoning processes.

Writing on participation in science fairs, Greenfield (1996) examined whether different gender patterns occurred with respect to entry rate, project topic (life science, physical science, earth science, and mathematics), and project type (research or display). She examined 20 years of participation in the Hawaii State Science and Engineering Fair. Greenfield concluded that 1) females are more likely now than 20 years ago to participate; 2) females' representation in the physical sciences increased over the years; 3) females continue to be less likely than males to engage in physical science, earth science, and mathematics projects; and 4) females tend to avoid projects based on scientific inquiry and experimental research in favor of library research.

Educators might have noticed that some females tend to avoid school activities. Males and females differ in their school participation in several aspects: selection of academic courses and vocational courses, and participation in extracurricular activities (Grossman & Grossman, 1994). Females provided with curricular choices choose fewer mathematics courses than males; the reason for this preference may lie with educators and counselors who believe in traditional gender views and so steer females away from mathematics and science, rather than with actual weaknesses in females' innate ability (Berkovitz, 1979; Butler & Sperry, 1991). Effective middle schools make sure females have equal access to all school opportunities. While professional educators never would blatantly deny females their right to participate, sometimes teachers and counselors unconsciously guide females in particular directions.

One study (Silverman & Pritchard, 1993) looked at middle school girls' experiences in technology education courses and their willingness to take technology classes in high school. According to their findings: 1) middle school girls appeared to enjoy technology education and to have confidence in their abilities, yet emerging sexism among peers began to affect their participation, 2) middle school girls felt discouraged from taking technology courses in high school, and 3) middle school girls willing to take technology education courses in high school wanted to challenge stereotypes. The researchers recommended placing high priority on employing more female technology teachers, providing opportunities for technology education teachers to discuss gender equity issues, and reviewing the curriculum (as well as the hidden curriculum that might slight one gender at the expense of the other) to make better education-work connections and break down stereotypes about careers (Silverman & Pritchard, 1993).

In secondary schools, increasing numbers of females enroll in advanced science and mathematics courses; however, their participation rate still does not equal that of males (Educational Testing Service, 1989). This difference may be less acute for females who prefer competitive rather than cooperative environments and for females who live in areas where gender stereotypes do not limit their participation. Females, especially those from working-class backgrounds, also participate less in computer courses, especially programming. One study revealed that although females constituted 42 percent of the students enrolled in all high school computer courses, 86 percent were enrolled in word processing courses and only 37 percent were enrolled in computer programming courses (Grossman & Grossman, 1994; Linn, 1985).

Females constitute over 90 percent of the students in cosmetology, clerical, home economics, and health courses and less than 10 percent of the students in traditional male-oriented areas, such as electrical technology, electronics, appliance repair, welding, carpentry, and small engine repair (Grossman & Grossman, 1994).

Females' participation in extracurricular activities also tend to be gender-related. Chess, science, and letterman's clubs are primarily male, while dance teams and cheerleading teams are primarily female. More males are editors on school newspapers, while females tend to be feature reporters (Grossman & Grossman, 1994).

Concluding Remarks

Schools, much like nearly all other institutions, have not provided an equitable response to both females' and males' social, self-esteem, motivational, and participation needs. Middle level schools have a particular responsibility to provide gender-responsive learning environments, especially since children form gender identities and self-esteem during the developmental years of young adolescence.

For many decades, educators, perhaps unknowingly, catered toward male perspectives and learning orientations. The late 1990s and early 21st century can be times of significant change as educators learn more about gender differences and gain a more enlightened understanding of females' and males' needs and perspectives. Change will take determination and commitment, but the needs of young girls like Suzy can be met. While gaining knowledge of the need to address females' differences represents a vital first step, significant change will require a genuine commitment to respond to the needs of female learners.

References

American Association of University Women. (1992). *How schools shortchange girls.* Washington, DC: Author.

Alexander, C. (1989). Gender differences in adolescent health concerns and self-assessed health. *Journal of Early Adolescence, 9,* 467-479.

Baron, P., & Campbell, T. L. (1993). Gender differences in the expression of depressive symptoms in middle adolescents: An extension of earlier findings. *Adolescence, 28*(112), 903-911.

Benenson, J. F. (1990). Gender differences in social networks. *Journal of Early Adolescence, 10,* 472-495.

Berkovitz, I. H. (1979). Effects of secondary school experiences on adolescent female development. In M. Sugar (Ed.), *Female adolescent development* (pp. 173-198). New York: Brunner/Mazel.

Brown, L. M., & Gilligan, C. (1990, April). *The psychology of women and the development of girls.* Paper presented at the Laurel-Harvard Conference on the Psychology of Women and the Education of Girls, Cleveland.

Butler, D. A., & Sperry, S. (1991). Gender issues and the middle school curriculum. *Middle School Journal, 23*(2), 18-23.

Crockett, L., Losoff, M., & Petersen, A. C. (1984). Perceptions of the peer group and friendship in early adolescence. *Journal of Early Adolescence, 4,* 155-181.

Daley, D. (1991, January 9). Little girls lose their self-esteem on way to adolescence, study finds. *The New York Times,* p. B6.

Daniels, J., D'Andrea, M., & Heck, R. (1995). Moral development and Hawaiian youth: Does gender make a difference? *Journal of Counseling and Development, 74,* 90-93.

Danziger, N. (1983). Sex-related differences in the aspirations of high school students. *Sex Roles, 9,* 683-695.

Downe, A. G., & McDougall, D. (1995). Effects of sex, attraction, and acceptance on children's help seeking and attitudes to interpersonal relationships. *Contemporary Educational Psychology, 20,* 129-139.

DuBois, D. L., & Hirsch, B. J. (1993). School and neighborhood friendship patterns of Blacks and Whites in early adolescence. *Child Development, 61,* 524-536.

Education and gender. (1994). *Congressional Quarterly Researcher, 4*(21), 483-503.

Educational Testing Service. (1989). *What Americans study.* Princeton, NJ: Author.

Felker, K. R., & Stivers, C. (1994). The relationship of gender and family environment to eating disorder risk in adolescents. *Adolescence, 29*(116), 821-834.

Fennema, E., & Peterson, P. L. (1985). Autonomous learning behavior: A possible explanation of gender-related differences in mathematics. In L. C. Wilkinson & C. B. Marrett (Eds.), *Gender-related differences in classroom interactions* (pp. 17-35). New York: Academic Press.

Gilligan, C. (1979). Women's place in man's life cycle. *Harvard Educational Review, 29,* 119-133.

Gilligan, C. (1982). *In a different voice: Psychological theory and women's development.* Cambridge, MA: Harvard University Press.

Girls can't escape sexism. (1994, May/June). *High Strides: The Bimonthly Report on Urban Middle Grades.* Washington, DC: Education Writers Association.

Goodman, S. H., Brumley, H. E., Schwartz, K. R., & Purcell, D. W. (1993). Gender and age in the relation between stress and children's school adjustment. *Journal of Early Adolescence, 13*(2), 329-345.

Greenfield, T. A. (1996). An exploration of gender participation patterns in science competitions. *Journal of Research in Science Teaching, 32*(7), 735-748.

Grossman, H., & Grossman, S. H. (1994). *Gender issues in education.* Boston: Allyn and Bacon.

Hyde, J. S., Fennema, E., & Lamon, S. J. (1990). Gender differences in mathematics performance: A meta-analysis. *Psychological Bulletin, 107*(2), 139-155.

Jackson, L. A., Hodge, C. N., & Ingram, J. M. (1994). Gender and self-concept: A reexamination of stereotypic differences and the role of gender attitudes. *Sex Roles, 30*(9/10), 615-630.

Jeffe, D. B. (1995). About girls' "difficulties" in science: A social, not a personal matter. *Teachers' College Record, 97*(2), 206-226.

Kahle, J. B., & Meece, J. (1994). Research on gender issues in the classroom. In D. Gabel (Ed.), *Handbook on research on science teaching and learning* (pp. 542-557). New York: Macmillan.

Koff, E., Rierdan, J., & Stubbs, M. L. (1990). Gender, body image, and self-concept in early adolescence. *Journal of Early Adolescence, 10,* 56-68.

Leder, G. C. (1992). Mathematics and gender: Changing perspectives. In D. Grouws (Ed.), *Handbook of research on mathematics teaching and learning* (pp. 597-622). New York: Macmillan.

Linn, M. C. (1985). Gender equity in computer learning environments. *Computers and the Social Sciences, 1,* 19-27.

Linn, M. C., & Hyde, J. S. (1989). Gender, mathematics, and science. *Educational Researcher, 18*(8), 17-19, 22-27.

Loeb, R. C., & Horst, L. (1978). Sex differences in self- and teachers' reports of self-esteem in preadolescents. *Sex Roles, 4,* 779-788.

Lundeberg, M. A., Fox, P. W., & Puncochar, J. (1994). Highly confident but wrong: Gender differences and similarities in confidence judgments. *Journal of Educational Psychology, 86,* 114-121.

Manning, M. L. (1993a). Cultural and gender differences in young adolescents. *Middle School Journal, 25*(1), 13-17.

Manning, M. L. (1993b). *Developmentally appropriate middle level schools.* Olney, MD: Association for Childhood Educational International.

Manning, M. L., & Hager, J. M. (1995). Gender differences in young adolescents: Research findings and directions. *American Secondary Education, 23*(4), 17-22.

Manning, M. L., & Allen, M. G. (1987). Social development in early adolescence: Implications for middle school educators. *Childhood Education, 63,* 172-176.

Meech, J. L., & Jones, M. G. (1996). Gender differences in motivation and strategy use in science: Are girls rote learners? *Journal of Research in Science Teaching, 33*(4), 393-406.

Nagel, L., McDougall, D., & Granby, C. (1996). Students' self-reported substance use by grade level and gender. *Journal of Drug Education, 26*(1), 49-56.

Nelson, C., & Keith, J. (1990). Comparisons of female and male early adolescent sex role attitude and behavior development. *Adolescence, 25,* 183-204.

Petersen, A. C., & Wittig, M. A. (1979). Differential cognitive development in adolescent girls. In M. Sugar (Ed.), *Female adolescent development* (pp. 47-59). New York: Brunner/Mazel.

Pollard, D. S. (1993). Gender, achievement, and African-Americans students' perceptions of their school experiences. *Educational Psychologist, 28*(4), 341-356.

Ramos, I., & Lambating, J. (1996). Risk taking: Gender differences and educational opportunity. *School Science and Mathematics, 96*(2), 94-98.

Roberts, L. R., & Petersen, A. C. (1992). The relationship between academic achievement and social self-image during early adolescence. *The Journal of Early Adolescence, 12,* 197-219.

Roberts, L. R., Sarigiani, P. A., Petersen, A. C., & Newman, J. L. (1990). Gender differences in the relationship between achievement and self-image during early adolescence. *Journal of Early Adolescence, 10,* 159-175.

Robison-Awana, P., Kehle, T., & Jenson, W. R. (1986). But what about smart girls? Adolescent self-esteem and sex role perceptions as a function of academic achievement. *Journal of Educational Psychology, 78,* 179-183.

Sadker, M., & Sadker, D. (1994). *Failing at fairness: How America's schools cheat girls.* New York: Scribner.

Schmuck, P. A., & Schmuck, R. A. (1994). Gender equity: A critical democratic component of America's high schools. *NASSP Bulletin, 78,* 22-31.

Shakeshaft, C. (1986). A gender at risk. *Phi Delta Kappan, 67,* 499-503.

Silverman, S., & Pritchard, A. M. (1993). *Building their future: Girls in technology education in Connecticut.* (ERIC Document Reproduction Service ED 362650)

Skoe, E. E., & Gooden, A. (1993). Ethics of care and real-life moral dilemma content in male and female early adolescents. *Journal of Early Adolescence, 13*(2), 154-157.

Terwilliger, J. S., & Titus, J. C. (1995). Gender differences in attitudes and attitude changes among mathematically talented youth. *Gifted Child Quarterly, 39*(1), 29-35.

Tong, J., & Yewchuk, C. (1996). Self-concept and sex-role orientations in gifted high school students. *Gifted Child Quarterly, 40*(1), 15-23.

Valanides, N. C. (1996). Formal reasoning and science teaching. *School Science and Mathematics, 96*(2), 99-107.

Williams, C., & Bybee, J. (1994). What do children feel guilty about? Developmental and gender differences. *Developmental Psychology, 30*(5), 617-623.

Williams, J. E. (1994). Gender differences in high school students' efficacy-expectation/performance discrepancies across four subject matter domains. *Psychology in the Schools, 31,* 232-237.

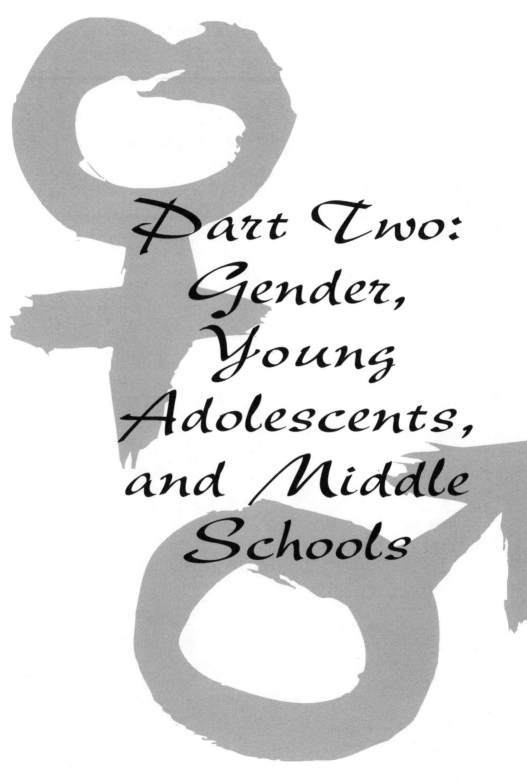

Part Two:
Gender,
Young
Adolescents,
and Middle
Schools

Chapter 3

Gender Equity and the Middle Level School Concept

As we have emphasized in Chapters 1 and 2, a strong connection exists between what the research is telling multiple audiences about young adolescence and gender issues, and the aims of middle level schools. Grounding the concern for gender-equitable schooling in the clarion call for middle schools, *This We Believe* (National Middle School Association, 1995) placed gender concerns squarely in the center of the middle school movement's urge for respect "for diversity and commitment to the ideals of a democratic society" (see Chapter 1). If, however, we look even more closely at the middle school concept in general, and at its traditionally embedded functions in particular, the middle school movement becomes even more clearly aligned with and naturally supportive of gender reform for young adolescents, especially as it accommodates girls.

What is the "middle school concept"? This is not always an easy question to answer. A couple of summers ago, a group of middle school teachers and administrators spent two hours in a session sorting through exactly what we all meant by that phrase. This definition resulted: "An educational environment in which the adults, students, the curriculum, instruction, and other program features in the school interact in such a way that the developmental needs of young adolescents, 10- to 14-year-olds, are met." The building block of the concept is the nature and needs of young adolescents, all of them—male, female, kids from different ethnic, cultural, or class backgrounds. Everything about the school is developed with an eye toward supporting the learner through this passage from childhood to older adolescence.

We were surprised and pleased, however, by the extent to which the concept had expanded in many practitioners' minds to not only include supportive curriculum and instruction and design of physical school components, but also to include the larger community of family, agencies, business—just about every other constituency that could be a stakeholder.

This conceptual expansion is heartening in three ways: 1) it recognizes the young adolescent's intellectual need to connect academic materials and skill development to "real" world experiences, and is thus still a concept grounded in the needs of young adolescents; 2) it emphasizes the importance of connections and relationships in the school process, and much literature on female development and socialization in this society speaks to this favored paradigm for girls and women in particular; and 3) it indicates that the middle school concept is vital, alive, and capable of change and flexibility—a hopeful sign for those of us hoping to make the gender issues experienced by many of these kids a more visible part of the concept. Indeed, the time is ripe for that visibility, given the middle level focus on young adolescent development and needs, and given the derivative nature of the middle school that is ostensibly designed to support them. The point is, the middle school concept in general is "gender friendly." The authors of *Girls in the Middle* (AAUW, 1996) evidently agree: "Key themes of middle school reform—connection with caring adults and active engagement in learning—are also key themes in successful programs for middle school girls" (p. 77).

If we push this synchronicity a little and look even more closely at the traditional functions underlying the school components deemed supportive of young adolescent growth and development, the picture of future gender equity in middle schools gets even brighter. The same six functions that characterized the junior high reform of the early 20th century also served as a bedrock for middle school reform over the last 25 years: 1) curriculum integration, 2) exploration, 3) socialization, 4) guidance, 5) articulation, and 6) differentiation. These six functions, which guided middle schools in designing curriculum, professional development, and other school programs, also provided an impetus for curriculum integration, interdisciplinary team-teaching, instruction based on active exploration of the world, exploratory subjects, advisories for guidance through the socio-emotional changes of adolescence, as well as other features now normally associated with middle level reform.

Do these functions and features co-exist with a schooling experience that particularly affords girls a gender-equitable experience? The AAUW Education Foundation's book on what works for girls in schools, *Growing Smart* (1995), espouses a set of principles for helping girls to thrive educationally: 1) celebrating girls' strong identity, 2) respecting girls as central players, 3) connecting girls to caring adults, 4) ensuring girls' participation and success, and 5) empowering girls to realize their dreams (p. 1). The middle school concept, with its focus on young adolescent development, its stress on appropriate guidance, and its recognition of the importance of positive identity development for all young adolescents, can help realize the AAUW principles. *Girls in the Middle* (AAUW, 1996) goes a step further, finding that specific middle school features like houses and teams, which can support girls' explorations of personal issues in a safe environment, and the increasing use of cooperative learning approaches all explicitly support girls' interest in certain subjects (p. 78).

And how might boys fare within a schooling framework that holds out the promise of gender-equitable education? As we pointed out in earlier chapters, many boys face obstacles as they develop and pass through middle school, too. Education experiences often reinforce societal expectations of boys, which results in failure, loss of self-esteem, and feelings of disempowerment. Connell (1993), in his revealing discussion on working class boys, agrees: " . . . the formation of masculinity . . . is more conflictual and more contradictory than older accounts of sex role socialization implied" (p. 204). The Sadkers (1994) refer to boys as "miseducated" (p. 197), also saying that while girls are shortchanged, boys pay a price, too: "Gender bias is a two-edged sword" (p. 197).

In a world that often views boys as performing at the bottom of classes, as having more than their share of learning problems, and as increasingly forced into strict male roles (often delineated by severe peer pressure), many boys need a school structure that encourages meaningful communication with concerned adults. They also need schools to be structured so that their academic needs are noticed and discussed early enough for meaningful intervention. They, too, need a school that allows broad exploration, allowing them to discover other empowering outlets besides competitive sports. In short, they need a school that can provide a more fulfilling education.

> *Many boys face obstacles as they develop and pass through middle school, too.*

Moreover, both girls and boys need middle level educators who are highly aware of the "hidden curriculum in sexual politics" (Connell, 1993, p. 205), and who nonetheless are "concerned with democratizing gender relations in the schools" (p. 205). If the adults in middle schools are not aware and do not work toward gaining equitable educations, they may fail to support this necessary balancing act no matter how good middle school reforms may be. They have failed before. As Tyack and Cuban (1995) point out, some historians believe that the earlier junior high movement failed partly because its leaders, more often likely to be male, followed the format of the high school, rather than the elementary school. The prestige of the male-dominated high school overshadowed a possibly more fruitful learning association with the more female-dominated elementary schools (pp. 73-74). Thus, the junior high became the "little high school," and subsequently failed to provide developmentally appropriate education.

If the structural features of the middle school concept support the needs of both female and male young adolescents, how do we make sure this structure permeates the vital interactive daily lives of adults and student learners in the school itself? The appropriate structures for gender-equitable instruction is one necessary item, but if it is not built upon or taken advantage of in classrooms and other school places each day, what good can come of it?

That is why the rest of this chapter addresses many ideas and suggestions for educators and their students in the daily learning environment. How can we use advisories to create gender-equitable instruction and teach kids about this issue, as well as their own gender beliefs and behaviors? How can we incorporate gender-equitable instruction in the school environment and related arts exploratories?

First, we must clarify why we should bother to try. Do we know if any structured interventions work to empower girls and boys differently? We already have outlined the findings on the problems and realities for both genders. What have educators tried that worked?

The Success of Intervention Programs

In recent years, many wide-scale experimental programs have been implemented to attempt gender-fair education. Most such programs focus on the plight of girls, since historically they are more likely to fall behind, academically, by graduation (Sadker & Sadker, 1994).

The Girls into Science and Technology Program (Kelly, 1988), an action research project that ran from 1979 to 1983 in Manchester, England, aimed not only to study the reasons why girls (including middle school girls) underachieved in math and science, but also to implement interventions (such as female speakers, discussion, career advice, and curriculum innovations) to determine which strategies worked best to change the situation. The program was effective in eliminating sex stereotypes. It also changed girls' attitudes toward science, lessened the usual declines in the number of girls who like science, and increased the likelihood of middle-class and more academically able girls to continue with technical crafts and the physical science subjects (Kelly, 1988, p. 88). While boys were not affected significantly (although some grew to hold less sex-stereotyped views of jobs), their education experiences were not negatively affected by the interventions, either.

While paying attention to methods, curriculum, and advising did have limited success in the Manchester project, Shamai (1994), concerned that teacher roles in overcoming gender issues in school were not adequately addressed, conducted an experiment in which 6th-grade teachers received workshop training in perceiving gender-stereotyped behaviors. Their own attitudes changed, and they actively engaged in instructional activity that encouraged student awareness of how gender issues affect their course preferences and choices of professions. Those students in their experimental groups did end up with higher aspirations for professional futures, and they at least had a more neutral attitude toward choosing a profession (p. 678). The study helped point to the importance of teacher awareness and training, and to the conscious implementation of gender equitable-instruction.

Even interventions outside of the regular school year have been found to provide success in educating students for gender equity. At Thomas Nelson Community College in Virginia, for instance, two programs geared for the average ability middle schooler, ATOMS and RSI (Remsburg & Buie, 1996), promote science, math, engineering, and technology interests, especially for females and minorities. Dubbed "Pipeline Programs," both serve a largely forgotten and "at-risk" group through a four-week summer program. About half of the students are female. As a result of attending, middle schoolers are more able to create a secondary curriculum that prepares them for technological education after high school. In addition, attitudes toward science are more positive for all gender and race categories, and attitudes changed in relation to science careers, science inquiry, and individual scientific attitudes (p. 6).

A word of caution is in order as we begin to review suggestions for middle level practitioners concerned with gender equity. While intervention programs tell us that creating our own gender-equitable schooling processes is important, such efforts clearly cannot stand alone. As Shamai (1994) pointed out, we need to "start at the beginning—the socialization process. . . . When messages transmitted to students in schools are not consistent with messages transmitted by society at large, the influence of the school's messages [is] limited" (pp. 678-79). We must remember, however, that ". . . the school is an important arena in which values are being contested, and, thus, lack of intervention means that the dominant values will preside" (p. 679).

So the attempt seems definitely worth it.

Gender Issues and the Whole Middle School Program

Advisories. Advisories, those often misused and misplaced parts of the day, could be powerful spaces in both young girls' and boys' lives. In a safe environment of trust, self-awareness and reflection, learned stereotypes of "female" and "male" can be singled out, focused on, discussed, and critiqued by both genders. Advisories, after all, are supposed to be the part of the curriculum that most deals with the socialization of young adolescents and their socio-emotional concerns. As we have pointed out in Chapter 2, many developmental issues exist that may prove ripe for discussion for adult advisers and their middle schoolers.

In a world where it has become increasingly apparent that schools often do not provide educational equity to both genders (largely due to widespread gender role stereotyping), where sexual harassment has begun to be a hotly debated and more visible occurrence, and where homophobia abounds, using advising times to carefully and sensitively discuss these issues could provide an important foundation for gender equity. Not only is it important, but adolescents seem to want these discussions; Davidman, Peterson, and Thomas (1996) found that gender equity was one of the seven most popular topics among 6th-graders! And a student's first experience of sexual harassment is most likely to occur in middle school (Vote, 1995).

As pointed out in Chapter 2, many studies show that, by young adolescence, both genders buy into conventional roles for women and men, especially when it comes to envisioning child rearing and providing for one's family. As if this were not already a formidable barrier, males seem far more likely by middle school than females to believe certain rape myths (e.g., women who go home with a man on the first date imply they are willing to have sex; women who act stuck-up to

Nearly one in three girls and one in five boys said that they were 'often' sexually harassed.

men deserve to be "taught a lesson"; if making-out gets out of hand, it is the woman's fault, etc.) (Boxley, Lawrance, & Gruchow, 1995).

The same study found that male respondents were eight times more likely than female respondents to believe stereotyped statements about women and girls; specifically, male respondents were more likely than females to believe that boys are better leaders, sons should be encouraged more than daughters to go to college, and girls should be more concerned with being wives and mothers than with pursuing a profession (p. 98). The researchers also found an association between rape myth beliefs and students who stereotyped women according to gender roles (p. 98).

While rape is at the extreme end of the continuum of sexual harassment and seldom occurs in most schools, these mindsets underlie other forms of sexual harassment, which usually targets girls. Born of these stereotyped attitudes, and often from girls' feelings of powerlessness, verbal and physical forms of sexual harassment create a hostile environment for learning. In case you think it is only a problem for girls, keep in mind that AAUW's study *Hostile Hallways* (1993) found that while over 80 percent of girls surveyed reported having experienced sexual harassment, over 70 percent of boys also reported it. Anne Chapman (1997), in *A Great Balancing Act: Equitable Education for Boys and Girls*, notes that studies found that "nearly one in three girls, and nearly one in five boys, said that they were 'often' sexually harassed . . ." (p. 20), to the point where such behavior interfered with their lives. (While not a study or set of recommendations specifically for middle level students and educators, Chapman's work is an excellent handbook of general research and helpful strategies.)

Research shows us at least one other reason why schools should deal head-on with fundamental gender-role stereotypes, and the behaviors extending from them. In a study of male and female peer perceptions at grades 5, 8, and 11, Hektner (1995) hypothesized that children and adolescents would find female peers having academic strengths and interests in mathematics to be less socially desirable than females oriented toward English classes or math-oriented males; the hypothesis was supported (p. 16). In particular, 8th-graders and males were especially prone to consider non-stereotypical females as less acceptable (p. 17). Hektner ends by discussing an important possible implication—that "the power of an adolescent's peers to regulate the social rewards he or she obtains clearly makes them, collectively, an extremely influential factor in the student's daily choices of behavior" (p. 22). This, coupled with the regularly noted finding that early adolescence seems to be a critical period for attitude development in general, begs for an intervention in the unobstructed formation of rigid, unexamined beliefs. What better place than an advisory period with a small group of peers, and a trusted adult leader?

While it would never be easy to deal with these gender mindsets, it seems that educators owe it to both society and our students to try. Other educators have begun to develop whole programs, as well as various strategies, to help educators think about such discussions with young adolescents, and we have tried to pull together some of the ideas out there, especially for those thinking of addressing this issue as part of these kids' development.

A Few Ideas for Working with Gender-Role Stereotypes:

1. One good approach is to show students how gender-role stereotyping creeps into our lives daily via the media. Based on suggestions from an activity section in *Education and Society* ("A Pullout Activity Section," 1988), consider holding a discussion defining "gender stereotyping," then, using a preset question guide, have students select two different weekly programs about families. They can come to class with notes, discuss findings in small groups, and examine issues of stereotypes and alternatives to stereotyped roles.

2. As Chapman notes in *A Great Balancing Act* (1997), the media, especially television, has real effects on students' behaviors and attitudes (p. 8). The media is notorious for playing up gender stereotypes. Making young adolescents critically aware of this aspect of media through discussions, and watching and analyzing bias-loaded ads or shows through a "gender lens," can help them develop critical viewing habits and perhaps a better resistance to media-imposed roles.

3. Once students are aware of gender bias and discrimination issues, and understand gender-role stereotyping, they can study how these attitudes affect both genders' course choices, career goals, and interpersonal relationships.

Some Ideas for Working with Sexual Harassment Issues:

1. Very early on, discuss the definition of sexual harassment (not all harassment is sexual).

2. Discuss the trials and tribulations of moving into adolescence and have students identify issues that they are wondering about or are worried about. Take these as discussion topics and hear each other's thoughts on them.

3. Have students write "unsent letters" to younger brothers or to boys entering middle school about what they should know about friendships with boys and girls, what they should understand about girls, and what barriers prevent boy-girl friendships. Girls can also write "unsent letters" to teachers about what roles they can play in addressing sexual harassment (Phinney, 1994, p. 7).

4. To pique interest and get involvement, give a Sexual Harassment Awareness Quiz, such as the one below, and discuss the results.

Sexual Harassment Awareness Quiz
Read each statement and circle T if you think the statement is generally true. Circle F if you think the statement is generally false.

T F   *1. Sexual harassment is a problem in today's schools.*
T F   *2. Men/boys can be victims of sexual harassment.*
T F   *3. Sexual harassment can occur between people of the same sex.*
T F   *4. One of the best ways to deal with sexual harassment is to ignore it.*
T F   *5. Women of color are sexually harassed more often than white women.*

(Excerpt from Strauss, S., & Espeland, P. (1992). *Sexual harassment and teens.* Minneapolis, MN: Free Spirit Publishing)

Add your own statements to reflect other issues you want students to think about.

5. Follow this by giving (anonymously) the Poll of Sexually Harassing Behaviors (below), and discuss the outcomes.

Poll of Sexually Harassing Behaviors
Use the list below to poll your class or a group of students to identify the number of people who have experienced these harassing behaviors. After you have compiled the numbers, compute the percentages for your class or school group.

	Number	*%*
Sexual comments, jokes, gestures, looks.	____	____
Touched, grabbed, or pinched in a sexual way.	____	____
Had sexual rumors spread about them.	____	____
Shown or given sexual drawings, messages, or notes.	____	____
Forced to kiss someone.	____	____
Had clothing pulled off or down.	____	____

(Excerpt from *MECCA: Making Equity Count for Classroom Achievement*, 1995, Overhead, 11-11)

Again, you can add numerous items from the literature on sexual harassment behaviors to fit your group. The data from the little experiment should uncover some revealing information and lead to some interesting discussion.

6. Be sure to discuss the connection between bias and harassment.

Ideas for Working with Peer Influences:
1. As an outgrowth of discussions on sexual harassment, examine peer harassment. Sexual harassment usually follows this more general kind of harassment, which includes bullying, threatening, constantly annoying others, frightening people, blocking or hindering, and irritating others.
2. If advisers envision a whole programmatic effort to combat gender inequity through the advisory, then faculty and student leadership training in this area could be planned. New Jersey's State Department of Education sponsors

two gender equity programs. One, ASETS (Mitchell, 1995), is a two-day intensive training program for student leadership skills, first in middle school and then in 10th grade. Both male and female students attend and learn, then return to school to sponsor the equity mission in their schools. Action plans are developed and put into action within the school. Such a program can take advantage of peer influence by having peers teach each other.

In keeping with the whole program focus, you might consider mentioning to your team the possibility of meeting with males and females separately to talk about the issues. Just be prepared for many types of reactions from your colleagues—from overwhelming support, to disbelief or lack of awareness, to, as Greta Phinney (1994) found, even anger. If formal advisory time does not work as a site for addressing gender issues, Phinney recommends initiating a club that functions as a "drop-in center" for girls (p. 6). This kind of group can function as a support group for girls as they move further into their middle school years.

Ideas related to gender issues that could become areas of discussion in advisories are far too numerous to be explored here, but include male and female communication patterns, eating disorders, self-esteem concerns, and careers. An excellent source for exploring gender issues through creative, interactive ideas is Utah State Department of Education's *MECCA* (1995), which is a large notebook and trainer's guide filled with well-researched, active exercises to help everyone (adults and students) become aware of gender issues and sexism.

Exploratories. In many middle schools, the students take several electives or exploratories per year, usually lasting six to nine weeks, perhaps longer, and every student eventually takes nearly every offered elective, or at least one in each area of study. Obviously, either advisories or exploratory studies are good places to examine issues with future career/work topics. In addition, exploratories in themselves actually help focus on one of the six foundations of the middle school concept, that of helping young adolescents explore not only knowledge, but also what opportunities await them and what possibilities for future careers exist. The possibilities decrease if young people shortchange themselves and their futures because of gender-biased views about what is appropriate for men and women to do with their adult lives.

We already have talked about this age span being a critical time for many developmental changes; mindsets are made or broken, and the self-esteem slide, especially for girls, begins. This is the age, for instance, when a girl may decide not to become a veterinarian, and instead choose something else that society has traditionally sanctioned as a "female" career. It happens too often.

In their study on occupational choices among males and females, 9 to 14 years of age, Awender and Wearne (1990) found that the ratio of boys to girls choosing traditional occupational roles was 8:1, although they also found that the younger the male (ages 9-11), the less traditional their job choices (p. 8). Providing a little more hope, their data suggested that the occupational choices of young females have changed. Most girls had a focus on a career outside the home as well as on a traditional family life. Many of those "outside careers," however, reflected occupations still considered to be female dominated. These careers are more "easily interrupted, less demanding, and require fewer educational prerequisites" (pp. 10-11). As we pointed out in Chapter 2, the mother's occupation and the father's attitude toward gender roles often help determine career aspirations. Worth noting is Awender's and Wearne's finding that lower socio-economic groups give gender-stereotyped answers more

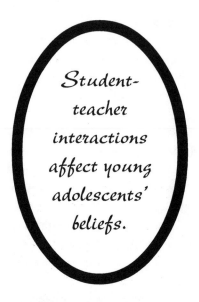

Student-teacher interactions affect young adolescents' beliefs.

often, followed by higher socio-economic groups; the most divergence is found in the middle socio-economic group (p. 8). The researchers also noted that work values seem not to change during grades 8 to 12, so the time for intervention is earlier (p. 12)—during middle school.

The findings are in accord with other studies. Morgison (1995) found that males do have more occupational gender-role stereotyping, especially those from lower socioeconomic levels (p. 58). In his study of career preferences for middle level students, Warren (1990) found that females tended to have more liberal views of occupation type acceptable for women than did males in the study. Warren suggested that students in the middle schools are actually the best targets for career education (p. 15).

Both the Morgison and the Warren studies found that student-teacher interactions could affect young adolescents' beliefs concerning gender-role stereotyping of occupations, and suggested strategies that schools and teachers might take to create more equitable views of future occupations. All three studies mounted a call for equitable education for 9- to 14-year-olds, since it seems that if students, males and females, can be reached when they are young enough, their already developed gender-role stereotyping for career opportunities may not become rigidly fixed.

Probably the best source of ideas for exploring work and career options, albeit focused more on girls, is the Women's Educational Equity Act (WEEA) Resource Center's Guide, *Exploring Work: Fun Activities for Girls* (WEEA, 1996). The approximately 160-page guide is intended for use with girls in the 6th, 7th, and 8th grades, either individually or in groups, as a complete and separate unit, or as instructional activities interspersed through other curricular strands. Some examples of the type of activities found in the guide follow:

Group One: Discovering Interests, Skills and Values
The "Instant Autobiography"

Lesson: One Hour (Group or Individual)
Directions: Use the handout to think about your own values or goals, or if you are work-ing in a group, fill out your own, share with a partner, then introduce your partner, using the autobiography, to the rest of the group.
Sample Questions:
1. *Name:*
2. *Grade:*
3. *If I could be really good at something, I would like that something to be:*
4. *I am happiest when:*
5. *Going to high school will be or is:*
    because:
6. *I think an ideal career for me would be:*
                    (Excerpted from *Exploring Work*, 1996, pp. 2-3)

This section of the guide has other activities, such as interest inventories, skill matches, and activities to clarify work values, set goals, and improve decision-making—all focused on a liberating vision of the world of work for young women.

A really good lesson in this guide is the one focused on fairy tales. This activity should last about one to two hours, and you will need videotapes of a fairy-tale style story, like "Cinderella" or "Sleeping Beauty."

Group Two: Stereotyping: Do I Have To?
1. *Choose the fairy tale that you think has gender-role stereotyping.*
2. *Read the story or watch the videotape, and note examples (individually or in groups) of gender-role stereotyping, bias or discrimination.*
3. *Then analyze it further, together or alone, using questions such as:*
    a. *What did the story tell girls and boys that they should be or ought to be?*
    b. *What forms of discrimination did you notice? How do you feel about the hidden discriminators?*
    c. *How did these stories influence you to think about gender roles?*
                    (Excerpt adapted from *Exploring Work*, 1996, pp. 47-48)

Section three of the guide takes girls through a number of options for careers and activities that spur open-ended thinking about the possibilities in their fu-tures. Activities place girls in role-playing situations where they use the scientific process (including astronomy and earth science as well as other sciences), prob-lem-solving abilities, spatial abilities, or investigative abilities. At the end of this phase, everyone might engage in the activity, partially reproduced here, called "Career Auction." This takes about a week to do in its entirety, and is too long to reprint here. A brief overview follows:

Group Three: Exploring Careers:
Over a week's time, everyone selects several occupations from a group-brainstormed and -compiled list of careers common in their region. Each person researches her lists regarding personal and material rewards of the careers and readies the information for the "auction" in which group members will bid on selected occupations.

(Excerpt from *Exploring Work*, 1996, pp. 119-123)

The exercise itself is often clarifying for those involved, especially if debriefing questions are asked and the girls reflect on what they have learned about the importance of the career reward focus.

The last section "puts it all together" for students. Girls can interview family and people in the workplace, select a female mentor in a career as a contact person, and/or tour workplaces. In all activities, communication is paramount. Here are some suggestions for working with a mentor:

Group Four: Setting Career Goals
Interviewing a Mentor:
1. *Find out what the mentor does in the job.*
2. *Ask what the work is like (a typical day, salary, etc.)*
3. *Discuss how the mentor got involved in this occupation.*
4. *Ask for a description of the mentor's view of the future of this career.*
5. *Explore the interaction of the job with one's personal life.*

A key component to such interviewing is a journal-like reflection, after the conversation, on what the answers mean for the individual interviewer.

(*Excerpt from* Exploring Work, *1996, pp. 140-146*)

Exploring Work includes brief readings on women, and culturally different groups of women, that educate and inspire girls to achieve (e.g., readings on women immigrants, black colonial women, women seeking higher education, and individual heroines). If you are interested in seeing the entire document, Chapter 5 lists the contact information. Do not forget to check with your state's department of education, as many have developed similar kinds of materials and activities, usually focused on girls, but also usually focused on middle schoolers. A good example is Florida's "Gear Up for Your Future: Career Information for Middle School Students" (1993), which offers a comprehensive overview of professions, and salaries and future projections for each career. Activities also include interest questionnaires, interview forms, personal goals question sheets, and decision-making activities.

Three Exploratory "Case Studies"
More common to exploratory curriculum offerings are three cases that deserve a closer look: 1) Family and Consumer Science, 2) Technology and Computer Exploration, and 3) Music and Art.

The Case of Family and Consumer Science. In recent years, educators have scrutinized the vocational electives in the middle school and high school curricula with respect to gender stereotyping. Historically, classes like home economics and woodworking or metal shop were gender-typed, and hardly anyone thought a thing about it. Educators in those fields have become increasingly sensitive to the more holistic needs of young women and men who are growing up in a world where the skills taught in those classes are equally important for males and females. Thus, curricular focuses have shifted—and often, so have the names of the courses. Chapman (1997) points out:

It is not enough to help girls acquire attitudes and competencies stereotypically considered masculine. Boys need to recognize the value and importance of attitudes and competencies stereotypically considered "feminine," not just in the family context but for success in the workplace as well. (p. 7)

In light of recent statistics, Chapman's words ring true: Fathers spend more time in child care now, husbands do more housework in dual-career families, and more men take family leave than a decade ago (p. 5).

Schools are trying various general strategies in order to eliminate gender bias in such classes. One simple approach is to require every middle schooler to take these classes. When many junior high schools moved to a middle school concept and implemented exploratories, changing each nine weeks or so, it became possible to ask that both boys and girls take, or "explore," a variety of topics, including home economics and industrial arts. As a result, the topics within a course of study have changed somewhat to reflect gender issues. For example, Batten and Feldt (1989) report that the Norfolk, Virginia, public schools developed an innovative consumer and homemaking program that was based on the developmental characteristics and functions of the middle school concept, and that it included a focused look at the elimination of gender bias and stereotyping. The focus on gender bias is found in some other curricula, and curriculum guidelines for home economics suggest an examination of sexual behaviors and gender stereotyping (McFadden & Monroe, 1992).

One good way to start an examination of gender issues would be to review the current curriculum and instructional activity with an eye toward asking: "Is the curriculum and instruction gender fair and equitable?" *A Guide to Curriculum Development in Family and Consumer Sciences Education* (1995), from the Connecticut State Board of Education, lists several prevalent forms of bias to look for in such a review: 1) *Invisibility*, or failure to even mention women, as well as culturally diverse populations; 2) *Stereotyping*, or portrayal of women in historically traditional roles only; 3) *Imbalance/selectivity*, or a text presentation of a group of people, such as women or men, only in one situation; 4) *Unreality*, or portrayals of events that gloss over discrimination or prejudice; 5) *Fragmentation/isolation*, or presentation of women's issues in separate sections or as additive components; and 6) *Linguistic bias*, or use of such pronouns as "he" to stand for everyone (p. 84). Obviously, the route to providing a more gender-fair curriculum would be to eliminate the above problems by using new materials that are more balanced, or by bringing in more materials to balance instruction, watching for inappropriate language use, being open about the past biases and examining them critically in light of today's changes, etc. The *Guide* suggests the following instructional strategies in all areas for gender-fair instruction: 1) making the classroom a welcome, open place for everyone; 2) making it a point to weave into the frank and open curriculum discussions about gender equity; 3) using a variety of methods (visuals, group work and cooperative learning, keeping students actively involved, basing instruction on student interest and experience) to get the point across no matter what the topic (in other words, honor varieties of learning styles and multiple intelligences); and 3) providing a variety of assessment alternatives (pp. 85-98).

Girls still shy away from technology education, including computer education.

The Case of Technology Education. As they do with math, science, and some types of vocational education, girls still shy away from technology education, including computer education, in greater numbers than boys. Numerous research studies highlight reasons why: 1) the continued existence of stereotypes about appropriate careers for females, 2) continued lack of information about careers in general, 3) the sometimes marginal place of technology education in the curriculum (Silverman & Pritchard, 1993), 4) the methods used to teach technology in the middle level (Boser, Daugherty, & Palmer, 1996; Silverman & Pritchard, 1996), and 5) the lack of same-gender role models as teachers.

Silverman's and Pritchard's (1993) study on barriers for middle school girls in technology education found that three other major roadblocks existed: 1) middle school guidance counselors agreed that students were not very well informed about career opportunities or always aware of the options that may await them in high school (p. 2), 2) girls did not make connections between what they learned in technology exploratories and future careers (p. 5), and 3) a lack of options to pursue technology upon leaving middle school. Often, middle school girls who were interested in technology could not find room in their high school curricula for these electives (p. 7).

More males than females participate in computer learning environments (Linn, 1985), and many studies document a definitive pattern of gender differences in computer use, interest, and achievement, with females less represented in classes encouraging higher cognitive development (Thurston, 1990). Often, the reasons for this disparity resemble those for technology education: girls and boys still see life goals as gender-related (in fact, the only technology-related class in which girls outnumber boys is high school word processing [Nathan & Baron, 1995, p. 348]); also, females' learning is not as well supported as males' by instructional strategies, classroom interaction and feedback (p. 3).

Thankfully, some studies have found that middle school girls seem to enjoy exploring technology education (Silverman & Pritchard, 1996). While boys continue to be more interested in technology, girls believe that technology is for both genders (Boser, Daugherty, & Palmer, 1996, p. 3). When girls do enroll in computer classes, they are just as interested as the males are (Hawkins, 1984).

The question is, how can middle schools build on this interest, developing it into a serious opportunity for more girls as well as boys? While schools can do more, especially in the areas of advising and guidance, the most powerful education medium for change remains the classroom. Technology and computer education teachers concerned about gender-fair instruction can:

- Give students, especially girls, choices about software options, making sure that girls experience not only safer "drill-and-practice" programs, but also more challenging ones that foster analytic skills (Nathan & Baron, 1995, p. 357-358).
- Give girls choices about projects. To paraphrase Silverman and Pritchard (1993), for example, principles of design can be learned from designing a house as well as a bridge.
- Recognize that emerging sexism among peers is heightened in middle school, and develop ground rules on acceptable behaviors that do not force either gender into stereotyped roles in classroom interactions.
- Create a balance between competition and collaboration, between individual and group projects.
- Make the technology classroom more attractive for girls by using posters or pictures showing women in technological roles, or by displaying projects made by females (Silverman & Pritchard, 1996).

Chapman (1997) adds several other ways to make computers more accessible to both boys and girls:

- encourage out-of-class use by all of the students by asking them to do at least some homework on the computer
- decentralize the computers, or house them away from the math department rooms
- involve parents, especially some mothers who may also avoid computers (Chapman, 1997, p. 26).

Overall, technology and computer education teachers need to develop "commitments to environments that embody an ethic of caring and connectedness—commitments that, as Gilligan and others have shown, are so much a part of women's daily experiences" (Apple & Jungck, 1990, pp. 248-249).

Outside of the classroom itself, some additional strategies for administrators, counselors, and other educators to ensure gender equity in this field include:

- Placing priority on hiring more female technology and computer education teachers who can serve as role models for girls.
- Considering special faculty training for computer education, especially for female faculty who themselves are often less prepared to incorporate computer technology in their classes. One good model to check out is a computer equity program for rural Kansas teachers (Thurston, 1990), in which they were given structured inservice training for a year so that they could provide gender-equitable computer instruction. Teachers taught their new skills with Logo-writer to an older math class, provided inservice help for other teachers, held mother-daughter breakfasts and computer sessions, and pursued other self-empowering activities.
- Scheduling technology and computer classes so that the number of girls is maximized in a section, at least to three or four (Silverman & Pritchard, 1996).
- Arranging for guidance counselors to work with technology and computer teachers, as much as possible, to help them help students see connections between classroom activity and careers. For example, guidance people might help teachers:
    - arrange for guest speakers, especially women, who can help break down stereotypes
    - Set up career days where women in these roles meet students
    - Set up job-shadowing opportunities that parallel a study unit
    - Arrange for high school visit days, when technology classes can be visited (Silverman & Pritchard, 1993, p. 5).
- Considering implementation of integrated technology education, one in which classes incorporate other disciplines (English, math, etc.) and in which other disciplines show their links to various technologies. In fact, this model for technology education has been shown to change middle school students' attitudes the most, both positively and negatively (Boser, Daugherty, & Palmer, 1996, p. 14), possibly because of its realistic and challenging nature. Some high schools are beginning to find that barriers to the old vocational/academic subject split can begin to be broken down with interdisciplinary programs (Silverman & Pritchard, 1993, p. 8).

Far from being a strange occurrence, this last suggestion is sometimes tried even now in middle schools that are moving toward an increasingly integrated

curricular day, in which not only academic subjects like English or social studies are integrated, but also the so-called
"related arts" and exploratories.

The Case of Music and Art. Surpris-
ingly, even subjects in the fine arts seem
to separate the boys from the girls. In her
studies on music curricular materials and
gender stereotyping, Koza (1994) outlined some discoveries about the past:
women of the middle class were expected
to enjoy music as amateurs, generally in
the home, but not to become professionals or public performers; some musical
instruments were more identified with
males than females, such as orchestral

Even subjects in the fine arts seem to separate the boys from the girls.

instruments; vocal music was thought to be a feminine domain, and instrumental
music was considered masculine (pp. 147-148).

In many ways, some of these gender-specific roles in music still remain with
us, as indicated by Koza's study on the presence and role of females in current
middle school textbooks. She found that "females were seriously
underrepresented in illustrations of music-related figures; furthermore, these illustrations tended to reinforce many traditional music-related sex stereotypes"
(p. 165). Oddly, it seemed that pictures of musical events, like choir performances,
pictured equal numbers of boys and girls even when, in reality, there are probably fewer males in choirs. Similar attempts to adjust reality in order to eradicate
stereotypes about females, however, did not show up (p. 167). Koza suggests
that we need a further examination of exactly how gender stereotyping is affecting the music field.

The absence, or at least the severe underrepresentation, of women artists in the
middle school curriculum spurred one middle school teacher to do something
about it. Noticing how few women artists were in her art curriculum, and recognizing the importance of providing women role models for all students, Mary
Lou Dawald, along with Janet McVay, an art teacher in another nearby school
corporation, wrote a grant (as part of the VISION ATHENA Two-Way Interactive
Video Distance Learning Teacher Grants) to address the issue. They studied
women artists at the Indianapolis Museum of Art (IMA) and worked on developing a "Women and Arts" kit for each school in the system that could be checked
out by other teachers. It was Mary Lou's intention to include the results of their
study in her own 7th-grade art curriculum. During the summer of 1997, Mary
Lou and Janet visited the IMA to research the museum's holdings of artwork
created by women. They also began taking slides, as well as purchasing books

and videos. Contacts at the IMA helped them locate women artists who might be willing to be part of the unit.

The following snapshot is an example of what can be done in an exploratory fine arts class (M. L. Dawald, personal communication, October, 1997). Mary Lou Dawald's students were in an exploratory. Each nine-week grading period, the classes would break off into three study groups: one group would work with computer graphics, one with photography, and one with women artists projects. Every three weeks, the groups would rotate through the other two topics within their class period, so that after nine weeks, each student in the class would have explored each area of art.

During the unit on women artists, students would work individually or in small groups. They would first look up information on each of the 12 women artists in the unit, then write a short paragraph about each one, including certain specifics about the lives of each. Then, each student would choose the one woman artist that he or she wanted to research more in-depth. This research yielded a two-page research report (word-processed), a project that the student created based on an imitation of the artist's works (sculpture, painting, pottery, etc.), and a final exhibition to the group or to the class. Samples of the unit work overall, and for each of the women artists, follow:

A Work in Progress: A Unit on Women and Art

Teacher Author: Mary Lou Dawald

Rationale: As art teachers looking to be all-inclusive in the art history, we find that most art curricular programs shortchange female artists. We have been making concerted efforts to correct this historic oversight and see the need for a unit on women artists throughout history. The middle schooler is at an age when he or she is forming lifelong impressions of occupations and gender roles in society. This unit should help our students develop an appreciation of women artists' achievements and their struggles in a male-dominated society.

Time: Approximately three weeks to one month, with follow-up throughout the year.

Major Goals:
Students would:
1. learn about different women artists
2. develop an appreciation of women artists' struggles and achievements
3. create projects and present findings to the rest of the class and to the "partner" school.

Resources:
Indianapolis Art Center
Women Artists Displayed at the Indianapolis Museum of Art:
French and American Women Artists, primarily from the 18th, 19th, and 20th centuries (at least 34 women artists' works).

Videos:
Cassatt, Portrait of an Artist, Vol. 2, Women in Art. Home Vision Video, 1977. Produced by WNET/Thirteen.
Kahlo, Portrait of an Artist. Home Vision Video, 1983. Produced by Eila Hershon, Roberta Guerra and Wibke von Bonin.
Nevelson, Portrait of an Artist. Home Vision Video. ISBN 0-7899-1337-9. Produced by Susan Fanshel and Jill Godmilow.

Books:
Women Artists, An Illustrated History. ISBN 1-55859-239-3. Edited by Nancy Grubb. New York: Abbeville Publishers.

Various Posters:
Lavinia Fontana
Artemisia Gentileschi
Judith Leyster
Mary Cassatt
Georgia O'Keefe
Marie Martinez

Learning Strategies and Activities:
1. Interactive discussions, via distance learning technology, among middle school students, high school students, the Indianapolis Museum of Art, a local women's history specialist, and a woman art professor.
2. Classes in both schools would use distance learning to take at least two virtual field trips, one to the IMA and one to the Indianapolis Art Center.
3. Study of each artist would include background on the artist, viewing of the artist's works, study of related art terms, and experimentation with the artist's style through the students' own creations.

Lesson Example One:
Frida Kahlo

Vocabulary:
surrealism
superrealism
superimpose

Materials:
12" x 18" paper, colored pencils, sketch paper, scissors, glue, writing paper, pencils

Activities/Projects:
1. Students should list three experiences: one of change, one of sadness, one that is happy. List eight adjectives for each experience.
2. Notice how Frida Kahlo's portraiture reflects her emotions and experiences.
3. Make sketches that would illustrate the experiences and feelings previously written down. Draw a self-portrait, realistic or not, that will be the focus of the composition. Works may be used as part of it.
4. Cut out sections of the sketches and compose them around and behind the portrait.
5. The final product should show feelings and state of mind, as well as a likeness of the person.
6. Each student should complete a review on Kahlo as a worksheet or a test:

Frida Kahlo
Student Name: _____

1. What do the three works of art on pages 2 and 3 have in common?
   _____
2. What was the first great civilization in North America?_____
3. Many Mexican artists became involved in political struggles and created art that protected against_____
4. Who was Frida Kahlo's husband?_____
5. What kind of artwork did her husband create?_____
6. Describe her relationship with her husband:_____
   _____
7. What health problems did Kahlo have?_____
8. She was best known for which of the following kinds of painting?
   a. Still-life   b. Landscapes   c. Abstract   d. Self-portrait
9. Why did Kahlo paint grotesque visions?_____
10. Write a quote by Frida Kahlo that best exemplifies her for you.
    _____

Lesson Example Two:
Berenice Abbott

Vocabulary:
urban canyon
straight photograph
cropped photograph

Materials: camera, black-and-white film, developing materials

Activities/Projects:

1. Create a photo essay that captures a sense of place. Select a location that has a special meaning to you. It may be at home, outside or some place such as a church or dance studio. Study the location from different angles, at different times of day. Look at the details. Look for patterns, shapes, and textures. Climb above and look down. Lie on the ground and look up. Take 24 photographs of your location. Process the film and print each photograph at 3 1/2" x 5". Select the best six to print at 5" x 7". Mount on posterboard with small rings of tape in corners, or a little glue, to present.

2. Students would do the following as a worksheet or quiz/test (samples from this below):

Berenice Abbott

Student Name: _____

1. What city was the subject of her photography?_____
2. When Abbott first arrived in the city, what were her impressions?
   _____
3. What was she trying to capture in her work? _____
   _____
4. Name three creative choices a photographic artist must make after deciding on a subject: _____
5. How and where did Abbott first get into photography?_____
   _____
6. Who was Eugene Atget and what did Abbott do to help him?_____
   _____
7. Of the three photographs on page 7, describe the composition of one: how texture, line, shape, value negative shapes are used _____
   _____

Other lessons, similarly formatted, focus on Georgia O'Keefe, Louise Nevelson, Mary Cassatt, Kathe Kollwitz, and Faith Ringgold, among others.

Unit Evaluation:

Students survey the unit once completed, and teachers conduct pre- and posttests on student knowledge/awareness acquired from the beginning to the end of the unit.

So that the learning experience will not be limited only to Mary Lou's classes, she, along with Janet, will prepare a full-scale kit based on their work and make it available in each school, as well as for the CEC. It could be adaptable to upper elementary and high school. Kits would contain videos, slides, pre- and posttests, resource materials, lesson plans, photographs of student projects, and evaluation forms. Note how dependent on up-to-date computer and technology use the unit is—in an almost natural way, since computers are the means to an end here, to equalize their use among boys and girls. And, as Mary Lou says, the differences are there already in boys' and girls' usage: "I have noticed more working in twos . . . at least for the girls. The girls don't ask me for help, they ask each other. The boys don't ask each other for help, but will ask me. Why don't they ask the girls?"

Extracurricular Activities and Gender Issues

Many boys and girls find a world of creative outlets through extracurricular activities: choir, band, theater, history clubs, photography, and others. These groups give both boys and girls, together and apart, a necessary ingredient for their development. In spite of Title IX and honest attempts to equalize athletics, however, boys and girls are still treated very differently.

Priest and Summerfield (1995) note that "although sports for girls and women have made great strides in the past 20 years, it is clear that equality does not exist" (p. 55). Schools are supposed to provide equal opportunities for both genders in terms of scheduling, equipment, coaching, compensation, travel, facilities, publicity, promotion, and so on (p. 53). Priest and Summerfield go on to say that "equity" may mean different things in each of these categories, resulting in disparity and inequality. For example, assuring equality in funding simply means that the quality of a program for girls equals that of the boys (p. 53), and sports opportunities does not mean that numbers of teams must be equal (p. 55).

Underlying the persistent inequalities are other, deeper societal conflicts over sports and gender. Chapman (1997) notes that parents, particularly fathers, initiate young boys into the traditions of sports and sports talk, and many boys are pushed by general societal expectations towards sports (p. 125-126), whereas parental expectations, as well as societal ones, for girls' sports participation is more neutral (p. 126). In addition, she points out that as the physical ability gap widens between boys and girls around middle/junior high, females' physiological advantages, which make them strong swimmers, runners, or walkers, are less valued than males' advantages of weight and muscle mass, which are demanded in more popular sports (p. 126). Finally, as the Sadkers (1994) point out, competitive athletics place males who are small, scholarly, or not drawn to sports at a disadvantage, as they are often teased, put down, or harassed.

Suggestions for creating a more balanced approach to athletics for boys and girls are fueled by the middle school concept's push toward popularizing intramural team activities rather than interscholastic competition. Even intramural athletics, however, with its attempt to involve every child, could ignore gender issues. At least the stance opens the door for more gender equity. More specific actions, in the midst of any type of athletic program, still can be taken. Priest and Summerfield (1995) suggest that each school conduct a self-study around the equity categories mentioned earlier and incorporate input from students, parents, and educators (p. 55). While this is an excellent start, Chapman (1997) points out a few other techniques:

- As much as possible, encourage mixed-gender teams and try to offer outdoor skills activities that require boys and girls working together.
- Try to place less pressure on boys while encouraging girls more.
- Help coaches examine the language they use in coaching.
- Try to encourage more females to coach. (p. 129)

This latter suggestion refers to the unfortunate loss of women coaches as Title IX implementation began to open up and make women's sports more visible. This change has drawn more men coaches into women's sports, thus reducing the number of women role models.

Service Learning and Community Projects

In the forefront of some innovative middle level programs lie service learning projects that, if well planned and implemented, have the potential to help both boys and girls traverse the rough terrain of young adolescence and bridge some gender gaps. Other than the potential gender resolutions or lessons, service learning has many facets of good education to recommend it. Halsted (1997) says: "The beauty of service learning lies in its ability to advance many different teaching agendas from workforce preparation to curriculum integration to community involvement..." (p. 2). She goes on to say it "should be a central element of the middle school curriculum, not only because of its obvious parallels to the philosophy behind the middle school," but also because "its instructional strategy meshes with young adolescents' needs and capabilities" (p. 2).

While Halsted does not address gender dynamics specifically, her rationale and conditions necessary for successful learning connected to community service rely on teachings and conditions that break stereotypical role definitions for boys and girls. One purpose she sees for service learning is to "foster caring, compassionate behavior.... Adolescents have impressive skills.... They are tender and empathic and rarely have the chance to show off their good will" (p. 2). One assumes she means both boys and girls, even though, as we pointed out in Chapter 2, society would have some boys define their qualities otherwise. At the same time, "Youth acquire skills, among them critical thinking, problem-solving and planning" (p. 2). These solid intellectual skills all too often are ascribed to males only (see Chapter 4), but may be considered natural for both genders if learned and respected within a collaborative environment.

The collections in our media centers must offer a gender balance.

The authors of *Growing Smart* (AAUW, 1995) also see service learning programs as projects with great potential to lessen gender stereotypes for both boys and girls. They caution, however, that for the consequent goals of leadership and decision-making skills to develop, such programs must not "confuse community action with community service" (p. 20). The former gives each gender experiences with problem-solving, chances to work for social justice, and experience practicing advocacy—not skills that young girls learn easily in many contemporary social settings.

In the same source, the authors speak to the potential importance of community projects for girls' development and empowerment. Community programs outside the school supplement, enrich, and enlarge girls' experiences. Community youth programs can be local or extensions of national groups like Boys Scouts or Girls Scouts, YWCAs or YMCAs, Girls Can, the Urban League, or Girls, Incorporated. In a lengthy report filled with recommendations for gender equity too numerous to summarize here, Nicholson, Weiss and Maschino (1992) explored how gender issues affected other youth development programs that were community-based rather than school-based. Their study closely examined overt attempts by various single-sex and mixed-gender groups to raise awareness of gender issues, and to offer boys and girls experiences through which they might develop a realistic view of the opposite gender and respect for one another.

Ultimately, the watch word is respect. If you are connecting your academic curriculum actively to either a service learning component or an existing community group's work, the outcome needs to be helping young people learn within a framework of continued empowerment, develop strong voices, and gain a sense of competence and capability. The result should be a mutual respect that crosses class, race, and gender.

Creating and Preserving the Overall Gender-Positive School Environment

This chapter addressed the larger components of the middle school concept—the whole school, its staff and their relationships with students, the school's relationship to the outside world, and the exploratory and advising components of middle school boys' and girls' days. Readers should also look at the components of schools that are least visible—that is, those "little" things that administrators, counselors, teachers, parents, and other educators can think more about, provide, and do to create an overall gender-equitable climate in the middle school.

Reflections of Gender in the Middle School's Physical Environment: The Case of the Media Center. In many middle schools being built today, the media center or library is at or near the central hub of the school. Along classroom walls and in the common areas (halls, cafeterias, media centers, etc.), visual representations of each gender at work and play send subtle messages about gender expectations. An all-too-common memory for supervisors of student teachers is that of watching a student teacher at work with a class in a media center decorated with posters of famous males. We saw one series of posters that honored famous 19th century English and American writers. To a person, they were men: Walt Whitman, William Wordsworth, Percy Bysshe Shelley, Ralph Waldo Emerson, Henry David Thoreau, Mark Twain, Robert Browning and on and on. Worthy writers, yes. Time to throw them out, no. But where were the women? Surely, Mary Shelley or Elizabeth Barrett Browning could have joined their ranks. It would have been a subtle and easy way to convey the message that both genders have contributed to the literary traditions.

As instructional designers, all of us must strive to provide balanced visual representation in the general environment of the middle school. The environment should be not only balanced in terms of gender, but also balanced in importance of roles played. It would not have sufficed, for example, to have posters of these famous male writers accompanied by one that showed "Wives of the Masters." Visually, subordination must be out; equal representations must be in.

Even more important, the collections in our media centers must offer a gender balance. Collections, often woefully out of date and very slim due to many years of underfunding, are clearly not equitable with regard to gender. James (1993) studied biography collections in two different libraries, one middle school and one public, and found that while females constituted 52 percent of the population, only 20 percent of the biographies at the middle school, and 22 percent at the public library were about females (p. 18). Certainly, collections should be watched for equity in gender of authors, as well as gender balance among subjects of books, fiction and nonfiction.

Often, the middle school teacher works as part of a team with the media center librarian, and librarians seek input on selections for the center. To be of most help in balancing collections, teachers and librarians might consider the following:

- Be sure that the books you order show (visually and in the story line) women and men with non-stereotyped behaviors, life patterns, and personality traits.
- Be sure that the books, especially the nonfiction ones, conform to non-biased language guidelines.
- Try to make sure the collection includes contributions of males and females from diverse cultures.
  (Adapted from Grayson, D. A., & Martin, M. D. (1997). *Generating expectations for student achievement: Teacher handbook*. Canyon Lake, CA: GrayMill.)

McCormick (1994), in her evaluation of instructional materials for sexism, suggests these guidelines, among others, for selecting library materials:

- Make sure books deal openly and accurately with the effects of sexism (and other "isms").
- Make sure both men and women, from diverse groups and backgrounds, appear in leadership and passive roles equally, in both work and home/family responsibilities. (p. 132)

In General, What Teachers Can Do. The first thing that teachers need to do is reflect on their own patterns of behavior and their own interactions with students of both genders in the classroom and in the school as a whole. We offered data in Chapters 1 and 2 indicating that teachers, both male and female, encourage and praise boys more academically and call on them more for answers, while they tend to help girls out more, as if they were not adequate problem-solvers. The gender research literature is full of observations about these phenomena, which helps explain why girls start out ahead in school and end up behind (Sadker & Sadker, 1994). For now, however, we will concentrate on what you can do when you are out and about in the school at large, not just when engaging students academically.

Many good self-reflection questionnaires exist that ask you to think about gender assumptions, beliefs, and behaviors. Voorhees (1994) suggests a daily "Yes/No" self-survey, such as the one used in her study:

- Did I smile at my students and reflect a pleasant and positive attitude?
- Did I make physical or eye contact with my students?
- Did I treat each student as a unique individual?
- Did I treat boy and girl students equally?
- Did I compliment students about their motivation, character traits, deeds or actions? (p. 131)

WEEA Equity Resource Center's publications often detail suggestions for promoting gender equity, including some self-reflective questions. They suggest asking yourself such questions as:

- Examine your own attitudes regarding gender bias. Can you remember instances of your own sexist comments or actions?
- How has gender bias affected your life? How might gender bias affect the lives of your students in the school?
- Who do you ask to perform heavy chores and special tasks, males or females?
- Who do you ask to do secretarial chores and special tasks, males or females?

- Do you display affection and displeasure in the same way toward girls and boys?
- Do you censure girls and boys for different behaviors? What behaviors?
- Do you (punish/reward) girls and boys for different things? Do methods differ?
- What are the behavioral expectations you have of girls/boys? Are these different? (WEEA Equity Resource Center, 1995, pp. 11 and 15)

Once you have reflected on your own attitudes and behaviors, there are some ways to call further attention to the contributions of both genders; for example, Mee (1995) suggests confronting gender harassing behaviors when you see them and watching language use in the classroom carefully, among others (p. 7).

In General, What Guidance Counselors Can Do. When vocational, technology, and consumer science topics were discussed earlier, the role for the guidance counselor seemed clear and supportive. But there are other roles associated with gender equity that counselors could and should play.

Carol Vote (1995) reviewed the counseling literature, asking, "Are adolescent females being prepared to enter and succeed in the world of work through guidance and counseling curricula and programs?" She concluded that in order to be successful, guidance and counseling curricula and programs must acknowledge gender differences and differential attributes. Counselors need to keep in mind the inner conflicts of the adolescent female and the real or perceived barriers for many females in confronting the world outside of school (p. 61). As in the case of teachers, she recommends that counselors undergo a kind of critical self-examination of guidance programs and counselor roles. Vote believes middle school guidance programs can be vastly strengthened through the application of critical self-review questions, which ask counselors to scrutinize: 1) district compliance with state and federal laws for education equity, 2) whether or not licensed educators (every professional) are required to meet gender and race equity goals, 3) whether or not parents are involved in career planning for adolescent females in particular, 4) whether or not counselors serve a co-equal role in students' educational development, and 5) whether or not the school improvement plan includes assessment of successful equity developments (p. 63).

In a similar vein, other researchers have targeted general concerns for a middle school counselor concerned with gender equity. Silverman and Pritchard (1993) call for counselors to: 1) help girls and boys explore non-traditional career options, 2) provide middle schoolers, especially girls, with information about the range of technology classes available to them in high school, 3) educate students about the level of preparation necessary for technology careers, as well as what are reasonable expectations for salaries and promotions, and 4) help develop links with the community, especially taking advantage of opportunities to bring in role models of both genders to speak about careers.

Vote (1995) also suggests that counselors: 1) have high expectations for everyone; 2) counsel girls to take risks, especially by encouraging them to continue taking technology, math, and science courses; and 3) select career aptitude or interest surveys that do not betray hidden sexism through language or role bias (Vote recommends using interest inventories that describe activities rather than listing roles) (p. 49); 4) try to schedule evaluations so that ongoing consultation and problem-solving occurs in order to continue to identify strengths, weaknesses, progress, goals, etc.

Overall, counselors should reflect daily on equity issues, and continually assess whether their guidance activities reflect and promote gender equity. Furthermore, counselors can assume an educational role with other teachers and administrators, reminding them to think about gender equity issues.

In General, What Administrators Can Do. The administrator's role can be every bit as important as the teacher's and counselor's roles. Like other education professionals, administrators should ask themselves some hard questions about their own assumptions and beliefs. They, too, should take a hard look at the school itself, its halls, media center or library, classrooms, guidance program, curricular courses, texts, and teachers.

It may be incumbent upon a principal to lead other educators toward an awareness of existing gender equity issues in the middle school. A review of the literature turns up several important actions the caring administrator might take:

- Check out the district's policy on gender-fair education and assess its level of commitment. Push for its implementation through efforts in your own school if need be (WEEA, 1995). Subsequent actions based on inservice knowledge and planning seems to be a key (p. 14).
- Writing in *Principal* magazine, Debold (1995) suggested that administrators should set aside separate inservice time for male and female teachers to consider critical questions such as: What does it mean for me to be teaching girls (and perhaps boys) at this time in our culture? What values and attitudes am I teaching through my actions? How would what I am teaching be seen from the perspective of females in my class (or males)? (p. 24).
- When you are forming textbook committees, have women serve on these review committees to examine the materials for bias (p. 24). Provide other resources needed for gender-equitable curriculum and instruction.
- The AAUW study on middle school girls, *Growing Smart* (1995), has several workable suggestions for administrators:
  - Run an assessment of school programs to find out what is working for girls, identifying needs not being met and developing ways to do so
  - Allow experimentation with different forms of grouping so that students have more opportunities for addressing inequities (e.g., staying with advisers or teaching teams over a period of years) (AAUW, 1995, p. 18).

One of the most important things that administrators can do is support the adoption of clear school policies and grievance procedures dealing with sexual harassment (AAUW, 1992, p. 19). It is not always a matter of reflection, awareness, good materials and instruction; sometimes legal problems come up that need to be officially redressed, and every middle school should be prepared.

In General, What Parents Can Do. The parents' role starts much earlier than the child's middle school experience. Even the most gender equity-conscious parents will find, however, that children absorb some stereotypical behaviors and beliefs from peers, the media, and social interactions. Parents can help girls and boys sort out issues with gender and gender roles. As Chapman (1997) says, "Children's understanding about appropriate ways of being male and female will be most heavily influenced by what adults around them do, . . . say, and how they behave towards others of both genders" (p. 138).

Rimm (1995) notes that females have benefited from significant changes in the workplace during the 20th century, and they will continue to do so in the 21st century. For boys, however, the most important changes may be in how they participate as a family member, and they will also have the "potential for new emotional expressiveness" (p. 4). To prepare boys for these changes, Rimm encourages both parents to be highly involved in the early years of the child's life. Boys, in particular, need achieving male role models to look up to in order to become achievers themselves. Tempering the importance of sports, playing games and doing activities together, encouraging them to take time with reading and writing activities and related hobbies, and helping them avoid activities or entertainment that promote gratuitous violence are ways that may provide balance for young boys (p. 4).

For girls, on the other hand, encouraging the "spirit of adventure," as Rimm calls it, is important; parents need to avoid overprotecting their daughters while, of course, keeping them safe. Girls need opportunities to play with mathematical and scientific games and projects, and with toys that develop spatial abilities like blocks, Legos and board games (p. 2). While the cooperative skills that are often learned in girls' traditional activities remain vitally important, competitive events, like team sports, can prepare girls for a competitive world (Rimm, 1995, p. 2).

The authors of *Growing Smart* (1995) suggest that parents assume an even more active role. They encourage parents to require the same effort and achievement from both their sons and daughters, especially in the areas of math and science. Start a family math club and make sure your daughter is part of it. Actively support a daughter's sports program. Get involved in suggesting equity programs that could be implemented in the school, as well as in forming support groups for girls, to help them face some of the typical problems of adolescence (pp. 20-21). Be as aware and involved and supportive of the potential gender issues for sons and daughters as you can be. In Chapman's (1997) words, "Parents can . . . become aware of the hidden curriculum that exists in the home . . ." (p. 141). It exists in the home as much as, or even more than, it does in the school.

In General, What the Community Can Do. Again, *Growing Smart* (1995) takes a comprehensive view, offering many suggestions for community leaders and policymakers for ensuring gender equity in the schools:

- Youth groups should provide mentoring programs for girls' exploration of non-traditional roles and career options. They also should provide speakers for programs in the school and make linkages where possible. If a recreational facility is provided, be sure that it is safe and supervised, and that it provides a violence- and sexism-free gathering place for males and females.
- Local leaders and school policymakers should be aware of school programs in general and their quality. Keep informed, listen to student ideas, note achievement data by sex, and provide funding for building gender equity projects or programs. (Excerpted from AAUW, *Growing Smart*, 1995, p. 20)

Across all constituencies, one recommendation is crucial, and that is listening to questions, complaints, comments—from both girls and boys. Then we must deal with them, while soliciting students' input on how to solve the problems.

References

A pullout activity section for classroom use. (1988). *Education and Society, 1*(3).

American Association of University Women. (1992). *How schools shortchange girls.* Washington, DC: Author.

American Association of University Women. (1993). *Hostile hallways: The AAUW survey on sexual harassment in America's schools.* Washington, DC: Author.

American Association of University Women. (1995). *Growing smart: What's working for girls in school.* Washington, DC: Author.

American Association of University Women. (1996). *Girls in the middle: Working to succeed in school.* Washington, DC: Author.

Apple, M., & Jungck, S. (1990). "You don't have to be a teacher to teach this unit": Teaching, technology, and gender in the classroom. *American Educational Research Journal, 27,* 227-251.

Awender, M. A., & Wearne, T. D. (1990, January). *Occupational choices of elementary school children: Traditional or non-traditional?* Paper presented at the Annual National Consultation on Vocational Counseling, Ottawa, Ontario, Canada.

Batten, S. L., & Feldt, G. D. (1989). *Model middle school program for consumer and homemaking education.* (Curriculum Project Final Report). Richmond, VA: Virginia State Department of Education. (ERIC Document Reproduction Service No. ED 329721)

Boser, R., Daugherty, M., & Palmer, J. (1996). *The effect of selected instructional approaches in technology education on student's attitudes toward technology.* Reston, VA: Council on Technology Teacher Education.

Boxley, J., Lawrance, L., & Gruchow, H. (1995). A preliminary study of eighth grade students' attitudes toward rape myths and women's roles. *Journal of School Health, 65,* 96-100.

Chapman, A. (1997). *A great balancing act: Equitable education for girls and boys.* Washington, DC: National Association of Independent Schools.

Connecticut State Board of Education. (1995). *A guide to curriculum development in family and consumer sciences education.* Hartford, CT: Author.

Connell, R. W. (1993). Disruptions: Improper masculinities and schooling. In L. Weis & M. Fine (Eds.), *Beyond silenced voices* (pp. 191-208). Albany, NY: SUNY Press.

Davidman, P., Peterson, G., & Thomas, R. (1996). *Good and bad topics for moral education.* (ERIC Document Reproduction Service No. ED 398219)

Debold, E. (1995). Helping girls survive the middle grades. *Principal, 24,* 22-24.

Florida State Department of Education. (1993). *Gear up for your future: Career information for middle school students.* Tallahassee, FL: Author.

Grayson, D. A., & Martin, M. D. (1997). *Generating expectations for student achievement.* Canyon Lake, CA: GrayMill.

Halsted, A. L. (1997). *A bridge to adulthood: Service learning at the middle level. Midpoints, Occasional Paper, 7.* Columbus, OH: National Middle School Association.

Hawkins, J. (1984). *Computers and girls: Re-thinking the issues.* (Technical Report No. 24). New York: Bank Street College of Education.

Hektner, J. (1995, October). *Sex-stereotyping of mathematics and English at three developmental periods: Student attitudes toward peers.* Paper presented at the Mid-Western Educational Research Association, Chicago, IL.

James, D. (1993). *Ethnic diversity and gender in the middle level biography collection. A scholarly study.* Unpublished Specialist in Education thesis, Georgia State University, Atlanta, GA.

Kelly, A. (1988). *Getting the GIST: A quantitative study of the effects of Girls into Science and Technology Project.* (Manchester Occasional Papers, No. 22). Manchester, England: Manchester University, Department of Sociology.

Koza, J. E. (1994). Females in 1988 middle school music textbooks: An analysis of illustrations. *Journal of Research in Music Education, 42,* 145-171.

Linn, M. C. (1985). Gender equity in computer learning environments. *Computers and the Social Sciences, 1,* 19-27.

McCormick, T. (1994). *Creating the non-sexist classroom: A multicultural approach.* New York: Teachers College Press.

McFadden, J., & Monroe, M. (1992). Middle school home economics: Curriculum guidelines. *Journal of Vocational Home Economics Education, 10,* 68-80.

Mee, C. (1995). *Middle school voices on gender identity.* Newton, MA: WEEA Publishing Center. (ERIC Document Reproduction Service No. ED 388914)

Mitchell, P. A. (1995). *Achieving sex equity through students manual (ASETS).* Trenton, NJ: New Jersey State Department of Education.

Morgison, B. (1995). *Occupational sex-role stereotyping in sixth grade students.* Unpublished masters thesis, Fort Hays State University, Fort Hays, KS.

Nathan, R., & Baron, L. (1995). The effects of gender, program type, and content on elementary children's software preferences. *Journal of Research on Computing in Education, 27,* 348-361.

National Middle School Association. (1995). *This we believe.* Columbus, OH: Author.

Nicholson, H., Weiss, F., & Maschino, M. (1992). *Gender in youth development programs.* Washington, DC: Carnegie Council on Adolescent Development. (ERIC Document Reproduction Service No. ED 362439)

Phinney, G. (1994). Sexual harassment: A dynamic element in the lives of middle school girls and teachers. *Equity and Excellence in Education, 27,* 5-10.

Priest, L., & Summerfield, L. (1995). Promoting gender equity in middle level and secondary school sports programs. *NASSP Bulletin, 79,* 52-56.

Remsburg, J., & Buie, W. (1996, June). *Community college successful intervention programs: ATOMS, RSI, and vocational gender equity.* Paper presented at the meeting of WEPAN on Capitalizing on Today's Challenges, Denver, CO.

Rimm, S. (1995). Raising and teaching boys for the 21st century. *Sylvia Rimm on Raising Kids, 6*(2), 1-7.

Sadker, M., & Sadker, D. (1994). *Failing at fairness: How America's schools cheat girls.* New York: Charles Scribner's Sons.

Shamai, S. (1994). Possibilities and limitations of a gender stereotypes intervention program. *Adolescence, 29,* 665-680.

Silverman, S., & Pritchard, A. (1993). *Guidance, gender equity, and technology education.* Hartford, CT: Connecticut State Department of Education. (ERIC Document Reproduction Service No. ED 362651)

Silverman, S., & Pritchard, A. (1996). Building their future: Girls and technology education in Connecticut. *Journal of Technology Education, 7,* 41-54.

Strauss, S., & Espeland, P. (1992). *Sexual harassment and teens.* Minneapolis, MN: Free Spirit Publishing.

Thurston, L. P. (1990, June). *Girls, computers, and amber waves of grain: Computer equity programming for rural teachers.* Paper presented at the meeting of the National Women's Studies Association, Towson, MD. (ERIC Document Reproduction Service No. ED 319660)

Tyack, D., & Cuban, L. (1995). *Tinkering toward utopia: A century of public school reform.* Cambridge, MA: Harvard University Press.

Utah State Office of Education. (1995). *MECCA: Making equity count for classroom achievement.* Salt Lake City, UT: Author.

Voorhees, J. (1994). *Promoting gender fairness in school curricula and classroom instruction through infusion of equitable resources, vocational programs, and staff development.* (ERIC Document Reproduction Service No. ED 389633)

Vote, C. (1995). *Guidance and counseling curricula and programs which prepare adolescent females for the world of work: Recommendations for the School to Work Initiative. (Review of Literature.)* Ft. Collins, CO: Colorado State University, School of Education.

Warren, C. (1990, April). *An exploration of factors influencing the career preferences of junior high students.* Paper presented at National Science Teachers Association, Atlanta, GA.

Women's Educational Equity Act Resource Center at EDC. (1995). *Gender equity for educators, parents, and community.* Newton, MA: Author.

Women's Educational Equity Act Resource Center at EDC. (1996). *Exploring work: Fun activities for girls.* Newton, MA: Author.

Chapter 4
Gender and the Middle Level School Curriculum

*A*nother crucial part of the middle school concept is the academic core—social studies, language arts, mathematics, and science curricula and instruction. In fact, a major concern of the National Middle School Association (NMSA) over the last half dozen years has been the nature of the middle school curriculum. While instruction certainly is not separate from curriculum, we will sometimes treat it as such simply to organize this chapter and its ideas about gender-equitable learning. Think of curriculum as the superstructure, the guiding focus for the instruction that flows actively in and around students each day creating learning activities.

Imagine walking into a middle school anywhere in the United States. What curriculum and what instructional approaches might you see? We hope that any of these patterns you see at least would be embedded within an interdisciplinary team organization. Beyond that, the curriculum could fall anywhere on this continuum:

Traditional, **Multidisciplinary** **Interdisciplinary** **Integrated**
Subject-centered

In other words, you may see: separate subjects, or separate topics or units within each subject (traditional); separate subject classes, with all contents centering on the same topic or theme at the same time (multidisciplinary); students and teachers exploring a theme together in small groups, or as individual inquirers, in unblocked flexible time during the school day (interdisciplinary); or the latter as the norm of the whole curriculum, with themes chosen from the students' relevant questions about society, life, or self (integrated). In any particular type of curriculum, teachers and students may be effectively dealing with gender issues, with appropriate instructional interactions and strategies (which we will discuss later in the chapter). Yet, as Chapman (1997) points out, gender even more often plays a role in the "null curriculum," which is the curriculum "we leave untaught without giving it a thought" (p. 13). Nonetheless, as we shall also see later, the likelihood of addressing girls' and boys' issues equitably in these academic areas may increase greatly when middle schools embrace curriculum models that are more interdisciplinary or integrated, a notion that suggests *curriculum structure* itself may carry an inherent gender bias.

Perspective One:

My Middle School Curriculum Structure Is Traditional or Multidisciplinary

Many schools still revolve around departmentalized subject areas. Educators may conduct a study hall or an exploratory, but they mainly teach one academic focus—their subject specialty. Some educators have an interdisciplinary team organization. They are grouped in cross-disciplinary teams, and they and their colleagues share common plans and groups of students, but they still teach only in their traditional subject areas. They may, and should, use team time to discuss and advise individual students, coordinate meetings with parents, make joint decisions, and create guidelines for the team (management issues, etc.). They teach alone, however, and talk about academics only within the subject department.

This is what we have termed "the traditional subject-centered curriculum." Here is its profile:

Traditional, Subject-Centered Curriculum and Instruction

Definition: Separate subjects or disciplines are taught for themselves, with their own discrete content and skills, during separate time periods of the day (Jacobs, 1989, p. 14).

Example: First period is U.S. history, second period is English and reading, third period is science, etc. Units of instruction are in each subject. Instruction could be active, but usually lends itself to subject coverage, with the teacher actively talking and giving notes, while the students passively receive the knowledge.

Curriculum Planning and How It Looks: The teacher sets goals, often using state and local guides, and more often adopted text materials; the teacher gets the necessary resources for teaching, times and sequences the units logically in order around the subject content, and varies instruction somewhat according to the students. Planning often occurs in isolation, or in discipline-based discussion within the scope and sequence of the content area.

Teacher and Student Interaction: The teacher is usually the authority or expert, while the student is the learner/consumer of knowledge.

Benefits: This plan is familiar to parents and teachers; materials, resources, texts, state curriculum guides are available; specialized content and skills for a field are articulated.

Disadvantages: This fragments the school day; there is little attempt to show relations among fields of knowledge, so it does not reflect reality outside of school; time is forced and not geared to student needs.

The multidisciplinary approach is not much different, but it does seem to be a very important first step toward the interdisciplinary approach. In multidisciplinary curriculum structures, the team has taken a further step in its conversations together and has begun to look at how to correlate the academic components across a student's day. Generally, the team decides on several unit topics or themes that they could use as a focus point in each separate class and agrees on a time during the year to begin and end teaching it. The following chart shares more details about the nature of the multidisciplinary curriculum, and about instruction associated with it.

Multidisciplinary Curriculum and Instruction

Definition: Several disciplines or subjects focus on a theme or problem, but there is no attempt to integrate those subjects (Jacobs, 1989). These disciplines might be related, like science and math, or could be unrelated fields that explore the theme, using the tools of each discipline. Themes would likely come from existing content generally taught anyway (Beane, 1993), and would occur for a specific time only.

Example: Teachers in an interdisciplinary team organization may agree to plan and teach around a theme (e.g., ecology) during the same three-week time period. English teachers may cover ecological vocabulary, math teachers may cover environmental statistics, and art teachers may focus on photography, while showing scenes of polluted or retrieved areas. Usually, students stay in separate classes and move to each subject on a schedule; classes seem related through theme only.

Curriculum and Planning and What It Looks Like: Teachers agree on a theme, which usually comes from a content concept common in the curriculum at that time, sometimes one that seems relevant to their community of learners. They agree on broad decisions, like the amount of time spent in the unit, starting and ending dates, and sequencing and timing of lessons; then, they implement the unit.

Teacher and Student Interactions: They may be similar to those in the separate subject approach. Teachers still tend to plan theme, activities, and resources, presenting those to students when completely thought out. Creativity of topic may inspire more project- and activity-centered instruction.

Benefits: This may be a good first step into interdisciplinary instruction because it leaves teachers on familiar ground with subjects, and motivates them to plan more together; it is generally more exciting to students.

Disadvantages: The students must make their own linkages across disciplines; assessment of student work is often still done by the teacher alone; it can mislead teams into thinking they have done "interdisciplinary work."

We find that most teachers in most middle schools see the world through these two curricular lenses. Evidently, much of the research on gender and curriculum and instruction does so as well, since many curriculum and instruction suggestions remain couched in terms of these specific and separate areas: math, science, language arts, social studies, and health and physical education.

The Continued Sticky Issues in Math and Science

As we noted in Chapter 2, a wealth of studies on girls' achievement in mathematics and the sciences has uncovered gender gaps in math and science careers. Educators began to address this gap in the 1980s, and a 1992 AAUW study found that while the mathematics gap has narrowed, the science gap may be increasing. Beyond this, some studies pinpoint the middle school age level as the period when the gap is most likely to develop (Blum-Anderson, 1989; Cai, 1995; Jensen & McMullen, 1994). Classroom researchers, along with other educators, know all too well that girls miss out on career options because they drop out of higher level math courses too early (AAUW, 1992; Sells, 1980). They know that females often feel less competent and confident in these two areas, and they consequently achieve less. But educators also see the beginning of a change—girls may be improving in mathematics achievement (AAUW, 1992; Cai, 1995; Chapman, 1997; Kahle & Meece, 1994), although the jury is still out about science, especially the physical sciences (AAUW, 1992; Chapman, 1997; Kahle & Meece, 1994).

In general, what can middle school math and science teachers do to provide gender equity in their classes? Some of it is the same as what language arts and social studies teachers might do. Be aware of potential gender issues, and assess your own attitudes and beliefs about gender issues in these subjects. Do you still hold on to beliefs that boys are more visually and spatially adept than girls? Understand that research does not seem to back this up (AAUW, 1992; Leder, 1992). Do you believe that girls are less proficient in problem-solving? Again, the research does not support this assumption (Cai, 1995).

Most important, become attuned to the existing, pervasive barriers to girls' success in math and science, while still supporting boys' interests. Studies now help us see how many barriers exist for kids at lower socioeconomic levels. Such barriers also hold back girls from many walks of life. Traditionally, math and science have been "sex-typed as . . . 'male domain[s]' " (Kahle & Meece, 1994, p. 545) in the Western world. This typing is pervasive throughout societal filters that girls experience, as well as in family beliefs and expectations. As we mentioned briefly in Chapter 2, the middle grades years, when cognitive maturity occurs, is when many girls begin to feel less confident in their academic abilities in science and math, develop lower expectations for their own achievement and, thus, express less interest in these activities. (Jensen and McMullen [1995] actually put it some time between the 5th and 6th grades.) By their high school years, many girls begin to take fewer math or science courses or they avoid certain types of higher level math and science classes. This trend can be very damaging to girls' mathematics achievement, and hinder their chances to embark on careers dependent on higher mathematics; it stands to reason that the number and type of mathematics courses taken is related to differences in males' and females' mathematics achievement (Kreinberg, 1989).

Through play and other outside-of-school experiences, boys tend to have more opportunities to sharpen skills and develop positive attitudes relating to sciences. Also, they receive more encouragement in this area from families and society. In fact, girls who are confident about the sciences often report that they played with their brothers' toys as they grew up (Rand & Gibb, 1989). Compounding all of these factors are teacher expectations and teacher interactions with students, which often favor males not only through unconscious assumptions, but also through teaching methods that favor boys' outspoken and more assertive verbal behavior—such as large-group lecture and question/answer methods, and certain kinds of traditional testing methods (Kahle & Meece, 1994; Leder, 1992).

Fortunately, educators have been aware of boys' and girls' different achievement levels in math and science for years, and so have tried a number of intervention programs, from which we now can begin to glean suggestions for teaching. Two early programs, *EQUALS* and *FAMILY MATH*, were developed over a decade ago to encourage females to remain in the mathematics curriculum for higher math courses, and to deal with one important factor in girls' achievement—family expectations (Kreinberg, 1989).

The *EQUALS* program, primarily designed to help teachers of mathematics bridge the gender gap, focused on awareness, developing confidence and competence, and encouragement to persist in mathematics (Kreinberg, 1989). Most of all, the program helped teachers develop a focus on problem-solving abilities (p. 129). Program developers stressed incorporating into the curriculum data about the workplace and the increasing options using mathematics; introducing role models in the classroom to model math-based fields; incorporating strategies for problem analysis and solutions—the use of concrete manipulatives, pictures, tables, diagrams, graphs, calculators, and computers—which all are used in estimating, predicting, and verbal analysis of the problems (p. 129). Most important, the problem-solving activity was the main thrust of the program's curriculum and instruction—not just a reward for the few who finished classwork early. Follow-up studies indicate success for teachers using these strategies:

[Teachers] described new perspectives and practices concerning problem solving and cooperative learning. A major difference . . . was a shift from an instructional style that emphasized the correct answer to one that emphasized a problem-solving approach . . . it was a different mode of instruction that impacted on the totality of their teaching. (p. 132)

Even more significantly, 7th- through 9th-graders' problem-solving abilities improved over these years; 4th- through 6th-graders experienced less stereotyping in their perceptions of math as a male domain. These students perceived math as more useful (p. 133).

The *FAMILY MATH* program, coming on the heels of *EQUALS*, involved families in the pursuit of math to offset their own biases against math, which tended to be passed on to girls and boys alike. It was a program "designed to overcome the fear of mathematics and to emphasize understanding and problem-solving instead of rote learning" (p. 134), especially for girls and minority students. Using similar approaches and materials, families and children came together to "learn and enjoy mathematics in a relaxed atmosphere" (p. 134). A teacher/parent team would teach in a school, church, or other community space. They focused on topics at the children's grade level, often on such things as measurement, estimation, geometry, and probability. The informal setting, the teamwork, and the parent involvement all worked together to increase positive attitudes, one element missing for many girls. Key elements in this additive curriculum include: 1) supportive environments, 2) introducing and developing mathematics content through concepts and activities, 3) an encouraging and flexible teaching style, and 4) a link to careers in the future (p. 138).

Both programs substantiated earlier interventions, such as one called *Multiplying Options and Subtracting Bias* (Leder, 1992), in which students, parents, teachers, and counselors were made aware of the relevance of mathematics to future education and career paths, and of biases inherent in the teaching of it. Students' attitude and willingness to take more courses improved as a result of this knowledge (p. 601). And, of course, taking more and higher level mathematics courses can be related to achieving higher test scores in the subject.

While one can read the above program specifications and glean from it a picture of mathematics curriculum and instruction that could be equitable for girls and boys—science may be a different matter. There is some evidence that interventions in science, such as giving girls more access to role models, career information, or a more interest-based curriculum, does not necessarily lead to their better achievement in science (Kahle & Meece, 1994). However, "taking specific courses and using certain teaching strategies seemed to improve girls' retention rates in optional science courses" (p. 551). Having teachers take an equity workshop may relate to girls' perceptions of competence in science (Kahle & Meece, 1994). Beyond this, some evidence shows that use of individual and small-group activities, if truly cooperative and not internally competitive, may be helpful in boosting both girls' attitude toward science and their achievement (pp. 551-552). Hands-on, manipulative materials that assist spatial and quantitative skills development also can be useful.

Rand and Gibb (1989) give us a better picture of how a successful science program might look. *Action Science* was designed for girls showing interest and high aptitude in science. This addition to the regular curriculum has been adapted by some public schools. At the end of the program, separated into grades 1-3, 4-6, and 7-9, the researchers found that the participating girls were enthusiastic, more confident in their own abilities, and more willing to take other science classes (p.

152). The curriculum had five parameters: 1) the class was female-only; 2) teachers and parents participated; 3) female scientists delivered the instruction; 4) the activities were hands-on, problem-solving situations using equipment; 5) and girls needed to have "fun" and feel successful (p. 146). In co-educational situations, Rand and Gibb suggested that some activities be done with paired girls so that gendered roles could not dominate as much.

Math and science teachers should consider several qualities of a transformed curriculum as they assess their own curriculum (and instruction). These qualities address not only content and presentation, but also teacher/student classroom interactions and teacher attitudes and behaviors. In describing successful out-of-school math and science programs, Campbell (1992) makes the point that these parameters could be used to develop in-school programs, as well.

Successful programs:

- are considered to be "not like school"
- are fun
- have many hands-on activities and projects
- focus on having girls do new things
- are relaxed, with little emphasis on competition
- provide opportunities for informal talk among girls and with women professionals
- provide time for questions, and enough people to help
- encourage evaluation of what is working (Campbell, 1992).

Pollina (1995) adds that good programs:

- connect math and science and technology to the real world
- foster atmospheres of real collaboration
- encourage girls to act as experts, and give them chances to control technology
- present technology as a plaything and as a way to solve problems
- capitalize on girls' verbal strengths
- give frequent feedback, and experiment with evaluations (pp. 30-33).

Chapman (1997) offers many suggestions. In all grades, educators should:

- summarize the new material to be covered and explain how it connects with previous material
- help students understand science texts by helping them see how these differ from narratives
- give untimed or take-home tests (p. 79).

Finally, Rand and Gibb (1989) suggest some interactions for working with girls, specifically gifted girls:

- do not help girls too much
- encourage girls to trust their own judgments
- make sure all girls can use tools and equipment (p. 153).

The Subjects of Strength? The Social Studies and Language Arts

Many educators consider that girls' strength usually lies in the language arts (and that the opposite holds true for boys). Shmurak and Ratliff (1994) found that "mathematics classes in our sample appeared to be the most equitable in female and male participation, while language arts classes showed the most male domination; science, social studies, and health and foreign language fell somewhere in between" (p. 63). Indeed, some evidence shows that boys do not achieve as well in writing and reading, at least until high school (AAUW, 1992). When one looks at the content and types of various tests, especially the National Assessment of Educational Progress (NAEP) tests, however, the type of reading exercise can make a difference in who is reading better. Girls tend to have better comprehension of literary texts, while boys do better with nonfiction text comprehension (p. 23), a finding that may simply point to the gendered reading selections prevalent by the time middle and high school begins for many boys and girls.

Other recent studies also challenge the assumption that girls are especially suited for the language arts (p. 22). In fact, girls' difficulties in developing writing, reading, and speaking abilities equals that for boys. Typically cited boys' problems evidently still continue; Sprouse and Webb (1994) found that teachers often exhibit gender biases with regard to handwriting styles. An illegible handwriting was attributed more often to a male than a female on spelling test samples (p. 17). Tests with illegible handwriting were often graded down simply because of that issue, and these papers were often attributed to males (p. 18). Chapman (1997) notes that boys tend "to perform significantly below girls in writing" (p. 89).

In the areas of writing essays and stories, and in discussions of literature, areas where girls typically excel, some hidden problems come to light. In a study on writing subjects for 6th-grade boys and girls, the Gray-Schlegels (1995-96) noted that sex-stereotyping was already noticeable on the parts of male and female writers. "Boys . . . wrote more often about males being in a position of control, with males as more active characters and females more often being acted upon" (p. 167). "Girls . . . frequently cast both males and females in positions of power and control . . ., and they were very consistent in having main characters acting with others, while boys usually had their main characters acting alone" (p. 167). While crime and violence appeared in both boys' and girls' writing, it characterized 77 percent of 6th-grade boys' writing as opposed to 40 percent of the girls' (p. 166). Chapman (1997) also notes that girls tend "to focus on narratives and literature while boys focus on nonfiction in their leisure reading" (p. 89). Just as in the areas of science and math, it seems that gender differences in style and subject of writing begins to appear at this age, if not before.

While girls are assumed to be readers more so than boys even at the middle school age, girls' reading choices may actually be a detriment to their self-concept and in other areas. Studies long have shown the different preferences in self-chosen reading for girls and boys, much of which is gender-related. More recent studies indicate this is still the case. Linda Christian-Smith (1993) found, for example, that romance fiction is most often favored by girls in grades 7-8 and 7-9 during sanctioned reading time in English/language arts classes. Teachers often defend the self-selected reading options as a way to entice reluctant female readers to read, reasoning that reading romance texts is better than not reading anything at all (Christian-Smith, 1993, p. 174). Christian-Smith's studies found that "young women's romance fiction reading is characterized by this tug-of-war between conventional femininity and more assertive modes" (p. 183), but that "the young women's version of women's assertiveness was a bounded one, one constrained within traditional views" (p. 183). She concluded that "teachers allowing readers to substitute romance novels for other instructional texts unwittingly contributed to the young women's opposition to the academic aspects of schooling . . ." (p. 186), and that the "absence of meaningful communication between students and teachers about their reading allowed many of the gender interpretations to remain in place" (p. 187). Thus, while teachers are dealing more with issues of constructing a gender-balanced official curriculum, sometimes using the National Council of Teachers of English (NCTE) guidelines for gender-balanced curriculum as a way to balance literature and other aspects of English teaching, the practice of self-chosen free-reading texts may be working counter to some of that gender awareness.

Imbalance may prevail despite best efforts in choosing texts. Finders's (1997) study on hidden literacies in middle school girls indicates that some of the strategies for teaching writing and literature that many teachers use, in order to be student-centered and actively engage all students, may mask some continuing and developing gender and class inequities in the language arts. (We will be discussing some of her findings under the instruction component in this chapter.) Evans's studies (1996b) on peer-led discussion groups of literature have found that the quality of the discussion, whether voices are heard equally or not, often depends on such factors as gender, cultural background, and perceived status. Her studies questioned the assumption that peer-led discussions were necessarily democratic; indeed, she found that they often were not based on those factors mentioned above. Evans called for close observation of these situations to learn how best to help both male and female learners explore traditional and non-traditional roles in an atmosphere of openness and trust. Clearly, related research finds that equitable reading and discussions do not happen automatically (Cherland, 1992; Davies, 1989).

Where do we begin addressing such issues? Some general structural answers at the curriculum level, as well as increasing suggestions relating to interactions within the curriculum, may help alleviate gender inequity. Most English/language arts teachers are familiar with the suggestions on gender-balanced curriculum promoted by NCTE. Some of the highlights follow:

Literature:
- Include selected literature by women writers across all eras of the curriculum, and study these in class
- Study books in pairs, one by a male author and one by a female one, on a certain time period or on a certain topic; discuss the different perspectives and why those might exist
- Do the same with film and video reproductions, or at least make sure they are representative
- Discuss the issues of gender balance in the curriculum at team meetings or subject area department meetings
- Encourage the principal and committees to work on these issues with parents, the community, and students (excerpted from Carlson, 1989).

- Give literature samples that force both genders to "read against the grain," which means they are reading about characters and situations that confront their own stereotypical assumptions about males' and females' roles; make sure that there is discussion and follow up to explore this confrontation in a thoughtful and critical way (Evans, 1996a).
- Help young readers develop the critical tools they need to see the political and socioeconomic interests that "can shape the form and content of popular fiction" (Christian-Smith, 1993); establish collective reading groups to discuss what they are reading critically, and form writing groups to write non-traditional romantic novels.

Chapman (1997) adds that teachers ought to include "women's studies perspectives to shed new light on the study of classics" (p. 89), or select paired novels, one by a man and one by a woman, around key themes (p. 90).

Writing:
- Experiment with narrative writing and then examine the writing from a gender stereotyping standpoint with students. Raise their awareness level (Carlson, 1989).
- Use other types of teacher-directed creative writing modes, but use a process writing approach to teaching them. These drafts can be followed by a great deal of time spent on conferencing, sharing, and exploring their own gender stereotypes across males' and females' writing (Gray-Schlegel & Gray-Schlegel, 1995-96).

General suggestions for handling whole class interactions would hold true for the English/language arts classrooms, as well. Calling on males and females equally, not gender-typing the type of classroom help that both girls and boys do, and carefully avoiding sexist language can all promote gender equity.

Middle school social studies programs have recently improved their representation of women, but much work still remains to be done. AAUW noted that in high school social studies texts, "while women are more often included, they are more likely to be the usual 'famous women,' or women in protest movements. Rarely is there dual and balanced treatment of women and men, and seldom are women's perspectives and cultures presented on their own terms" (AAUW, 1992, p. 62). The situation is similar for middle school texts.

But none of this addresses the content of study on a daily basis as teachers talk with students and students with other students about the important issues and events in history or other social sciences. To a large extent, social studies remains focused on political events and issues, and on historical chronology. The focus on inventions, politics, and military actions tends to highlight men's roles in society. So do social studies tests. It is no wonder that "girls . . . do substantially less well than boys overall on standard history tests" (Chapman, 1997, p. 56). Women's place in history or women's issues are rarely noted, except perhaps during a women's history month, if that gets more than a passing nod of notice. As Chapman (1997) points out, "middle class white boys . . . also need the history of women . . . so they can have an accurate understanding of and empathy with, the 'others' to whom they will be relating" (p. 55).

What can any teacher or educator do about the continuing neglect of females' perspectives in social sciences, particularly history? Starting with observed and accepted "months" could be a way to make visible the content and issues of women in the social sciences and educators can expand from there. Mary Pence Greely (1992) speaks of her experiences in expanding the views of her students by building on her state's essay contest on women's issues during the month of March (in spite of decreased funding for such activities). Building on this month's visibility, she and colleagues developed a "history bee" around a list of famous, and not-so-famous, women. This list was given to each student and a second list was annotated by history, English, and art teachers. Students were asked to identify the women from a fact or clue during the bee (p. 30). This activity expanded into a daily question for each class on women and history. Posters about women were developed and displayed in various parts of the school, and various women's history bulletin boards were created. Library support extended to posters and featured books on women and the past. In addition, in the regular curricula, teachers made efforts to teach more about individual women's contributions, in different eras, to a particular discipline. Some students embarked on individual research projects, writing about women from their own families (p. 30). Women's issues gained visibility and spread from the social sciences arena into more interdisciplinary areas.

Voorhees (1994) had similar success in building on existing women's history months to expand the visibility of, and knowledge about, women in literature and history. Women's history activities began with the development of several school-wide bulletin boards highlighting women's accomplishments across the curricular areas. An essay contest on women emerged as a vehicle to continue the awareness, as did variously interspersed assemblies in which outside speakers offered little-known information about women and their roles in history. Topics included women spies in the Civil War and suffragettes. Teams of students researched and created projects related to women in history. To help further connect the learning across the disciplines, the school invited several local female artists to speak to students (p. 157). Actually, Voorhees's project was a comprehensive set of interventions reaching beyond history and other social sciences; teachers learned new teaching techniques designed to promote inclusiveness, and developed committees to plan for and assess increasing attention to gender issues.

Both these approaches naturally built on existing efforts to improve the social sciences curriculum (especially history). Awareness of existing issues and the will to transform "the way things are" are important in this kind of curriculum change. Increasingly, teachers' social science materials, in the form of kits, methods texts, and consumable materials, already do focus on women and women of color, so the job is not quite as hard as it once might have been. It becomes even less difficult as teachers on teams representing different subjects begin to see the possible connections through women's issues and contributions.

In addition, more equitable ways of approaching teaching history in particular appear in general pedagogical texts for teachers. *A Great Balancing Act* (Chapman, 1997) and *Creating the Non-Sexist Classroom* (McCormick, 1994) are two texts offering teaching ideas that apply to social science topics more broadly. These ideas may serve to spur more thinking about equitable strategies in these fields.

The Current Story of Health and Physical Education

As we pointed out in Chapter 2, adolescents' health concerns, ranging from the normalcy of radical physical changes, and the consequent, for some, emotional and physical reactions (e.g., depression, early alcohol or drug use, stress, or eating disorders), supply an abiding rationale for a good health (and physical education) curriculum. A wealth of topics can be explored. First, what seems to be the current status of middle school health and physical education?

Just as with athletics, Title IX had a great impact on these subjects. Of course, Title IX said that physical education opportunities must be open to all, as well as being equal in other ways; classes were to be integrated for instruction (Lirgg, 1993). In spite of attempts through Title IX and general societal awareness of gender and physical education, some research continues to demonstrate that, at least among 5th-graders, girls' choices of physical activity at recess are already more limited and tend to be more passive and non-competitive, compared to boys' opportunities and choices (Twarek & George, 1994).

Most research generally calls for coeducation health and physical education classes based on performance tests and achievement tests (Lirgg, 1993), in spite of some gender differences in engagement with physical education or activity. Lirgg found that coeducational classes positively affected boys' confidence levels, more than same-sex classes did. Girls' confidence levels were not affected, however, despite a suggested trend toward more confidence in same-sex classes. In other words, girls may not use a social comparison process (as boys may do) to determine self-confidence, and they may even define success differently (not as skills achieved, but rather as effort expended) (p. 332).

What such studies suggest is that the implementation of law and policy may not translate readily into automatic solutions for equity. Educators need to monitor classes and determine the best options for students, whether they be single-sex or coeducational classes. In other words, as Lirgg (1993) suggests, "the best physical education situation may not be clearly identified" (p. 333). Thus, educators need to be open to varied formats.

Educators also need to be open about health issues for both genders. McCormick (1994) offers several ideas for health and physical education that help students become more conscious of the roles played by gender and culture in their own health and development:

- have students analyze different family patterns and assess possible effects on the future health care of women
- discuss the effects of Title IX on physical education, having students monitor local newspaper coverage of male and female sports
- research and discuss different forms of health care and their relationships to gender and culture. (pp. 100-101)

Both health and physical education teachers need to help all middle schoolers appreciate not only the inevitable changes affecting them, but also the meanings that they attach to these changes, as well as how those meanings are often culturally and socially constructed.

Ideas for Multidisciplinary Connections with Gender in Mind

A multidisciplinary curriculum becomes not only highly possible, but perhaps even quite likely, when middle school curricula broaden to include gender-responsive studies. Here is a unit idea for correlated curriculum teams:

A Multidisciplinary Unit Around Women's History Month. In keeping with the use of extant months or celebrations, a team could determine to focus on balancing women and men in their curriculum areas. The English/language arts teacher might plan literary selections that provide a balanced representation of women and men poets, novelists, short story authors, and dramatists, as well as nonfiction writers. A further dimension of this effort might be including written reflections on being a woman or a man during certain times of history.

The social studies teacher could plan to include studies of women in politics, as well as a history of women's issues in the 19th and 20th centuries. Topics in history might focus more on social history and sociological topics, such as the changing nature of the family and women's roles in work.

Science and math teachers might focus part of their time on women inventors and contributors to their fields, and they could make women's issues a focus of their particular discipline. Problem-solving in mathematics could focus on problems relating to women's incomes vs. men's, or on gender-specific work statistics, and how these changed over time. Statistics problems could be based on defining women's participation in the workforce, or on other family-related statistics. Science topics, such as biology, could include studies of male and female health issues and how they are affected by biological makeup. Studies of population issues (biology or social issues) also could be done during this set-aside time.

The health and physical education teacher could introduce students to the history of both men's and women's sports and physical education, and students could study the political, biological and social reasons behind the separation of men's and women's sports. Cross-gender physical activities could implemented.

Of course, many more disciplinary topics in each field can be drawn upon if the focus is, at least in part, on gender issues. In the true multidisciplinary fashion, teams of students and teachers would probably continue to meet in their normally scheduled time and keep their teaching separate, but curriculum continuity would continue across much of the student's day. Team planning would occur during the in-common planning time. Many more ideas are possible and many adjustments could be made as the month of study progressed.

Perspective Two:
My Middle School Curriculum Structure Is Interdisciplinary or Integrated
In a 1991 article for the *Middle School Journal*, Butler and Sperry argued that if the middle level curriculum (and instructional practice) was to be firmly grounded in the development of the young adolescent, and if early adolescence poses slightly different developmental challenges for girls and boys, then middle school educators need to think carefully about implementing a curriculum and instruction that would enhance girls' learning as well as boys' (p. 21). They posited that the middle school's implementation of a truly interdisciplinary or integrated curriculum, using appropriate instructional strategies, might meet both goals. Others before them seemed to agree. Voorhees (1994) reminds us of Shakeshaft, Gilligan and Pierce's (1986) observation, which is good to keep in mind when thinking of curriculum and instruction, that "not only are the goals of schooling primarily male and public, but the process by which knowledge is transferred in schools is based on male development" (Voorhees, 1994, p. 39). The basic attributes of the interdisciplinary unit and the integrated curriculum follow:

Interdisciplinary Curriculum and Instruction

Definition: A curriculum and instruction unit that consciously applies methods, concepts, skills, and language from more than one discipline to examine, in an interdependent way, a central theme, issue, problem, topic, or experience (Jacobs, 1989). Often, this is achieved by studying an issue or a problem by using a discovery, problem-solving, or inquiry focus. This kind of curriculum and instruction is a shift in thinking, because it allows students to see how contents interrelate, and how they are part of a larger whole or framework.

Example: Periodically, the full range of disciplines in the school curriculum is deliberately brought together to provide multiple perspectives on a theme or issue, usually for a short period of time, since these are still embedded within the regular curriculum structure. A student studying an interdisciplinary unit on her home town, for example, may work on a project in which she traces crime patterns over the last century. She uses historical skills learned in social studies to research records; plans interview questions that she learned in Language Arts; uses graphing skills, numbers, and formulas from math to determine changes over time, and includes a section on how certain scientific changes in the last century may have influenced crime patterns or methods. She further develops writing skills and understanding of expository text in completing a report. She may even engage in prediction, using her data. Time may be scheduled differently for a shorter unit.

Curriculum Planning and How It Looks: It may look much the same as multidisciplinary planning. The teachers still control the topics and plan many of the activities and the scheduling, but the students may have input and choices on what they study in detail. Often, there is a culminating event for the end of the unit, for celebrating and sharing.

Student and Teacher Interactions: These are less passive learning modes for students than the two aforementioned models. Most IDUs are more project- and activity-oriented, especially since many depend on student-generated creative or problem-solution outcomes. There tends to be more group work, more individual conferencing and more assistance from the teacher—leading to a balance of activities, including whole-group and teacher-centered activities.

Benefits: It permits greater student involvement and motivation; allows students to apply their learning in various subjects more than under traditional study; students may begin to see relatedness of subjects.

Disadvantages: Some subjects may not be as well suited as others to the unit topic or theme; possible loss of identity with subject area colleagues.

Integrated Curriculum and Instruction

Definition: A curriculum and instruction mode in which subject boundaries are blurred, possibly even dissolved (Brazee & Capelluti, 1995). Traditional subjects cease to be the organizing centers of study, as do totally teacher- and content-determined themes. Instead, the organizing center of the curriculum becomes personal/social concerns and issues important to young adolescents, all of which cross subject lines (Beane, 1993). Important concepts, skills, content, and attitudes are studied from various disciplines as they naturally arise from the unit context. (When the curriculum becomes fully composed of the authentic questions and issues of young adolescents, what Beane would call a "general" curriculum (1993), Brazee and Capelluti (1995) call it an integrative curriculum.)

Example: Students' school day is not fragmented by subject area. Large blocks of time are available during the day to work on authentic curriculum topics either in groups, by oneself, with teachers, or with others in the community, and to do activities and engage in meaningful thinking, discussion, and action that solves problems or answers key or critical questions.

Curriculum and Planning and How It Looks: Unlike in the other models, the teachers may choose the planning frameworks, although these are consciously chosen to deal with young adolescents' needs and interests. Planning of curriculum topics, directions, and activities is done fully and collaboratively with teachers and students.

Teacher and Student Interactions: The students' role becomes the least passive of all the possible options, because their input is present from the beginning of the learning process. Activity becomes even more like that described under interdisciplinary, and characterizes the time spent in school, not just for isolated periods. Teachers work more equally with students, although they still set up frameworks and make decisions. They are not disseminators of knowledge, but rather are facilitators in students' search for self and social meaning (Beane, 1993). Power shifts have occurred, in terms of deciding who defines what knowledge is worth knowing.

Benefits: This is more like real life, in that learning is natural because it is contextual; motivation becomes intrinsic because people are pursuing real questions, issues, and concerns; student and teacher ownership is more possible; scheduling, blocking time and students, and assessments all change (becoming more geared to performance).

Disadvantages: A paradigm shift is required for full integration to occur; it is difficult to explain where and how content, skills, etc. will be learned, especially to parents and other non-educators.

Note that both types of curriculum assume, as did multidisciplinary curricula, that teams are actively engaged in curriculum and instruction planning. These latter two curricula also are characterized by a focus on such attributes as: 1) student-centered activities, collaborative group work, individual inquiries, real problem-solving, and more performance-oriented student assessment; 2) a sense that the responsibility for learning lies with the student; 3) a redefinition of the role of teacher to one of guide and facilitator of the learning, and perhaps as resource person; 4) highly flexible use of time during the day, which is driven by the curriculum rather than the schedule driving the curriculum; 5) a tendency to connect with real problems in students' lives and in their communities, thus leading to a tendency to draw from parent and community resources; and 6) a curriculum organized on problems, social issues, or themes rather than on the discipline of study itself.

A comparison of these key characteristics uncovers striking similarities with the increasing number of descriptions available about gender-equitable or -responsive curricula, especially those focusing on a curricular structure that enhances fairness for females. Mandates for gender reform from the 1990 report in *Outlook* (Restructuring Education, 1990) overlap the descriptions above closely; they suggest an entire "restructuring of schools" to promote gender fairness, which includes: 1) the abandonment of tracking; 2) a curriculum reflecting common themes; 3) interdisciplinary teaching that tackles real-world problems, combined with hands-on projects; and 4) a multicultural approach to subjects that shows women and minorities as leaders and decision-makers in the world (pp. 3-5).

Gender equity guidelines from state departments show similarity to the curricular and instructional characteristics of interdisciplinary and integrated curricula. For example, the State of Connecticut's guidelines for family and consumer sciences curriculum development (Connecticut State Board of Education, 1995) includes an overview of broader, non-subject specific, gender-fair and multicultural curriculum components, which are: 1) use of local community resources; 2) inclusion of a range of activities based on multiple and differing learning styles; 3) coordination of content, attitudes, and skills across the curriculum; 4) linkage to performance-based alternative assessments (pp. 85-86).

Perhaps the most striking synchronization arises from reading a feminist perspective on curriculum and instruction. Peggy McIntosh describes her work with curriculum revision involving Women's Studies, and finds five basic curriculum change phases that occur as educators go about revisioning their curricula, virtually in any field (McIntosh, 1983). Each phase is increasingly more transformative of traditional curricular structure. In Phases One through Three, women and their contributions to humanity are either totally absent ("womanless"), are included only as they are "notable" within the field, or are included as part of a challenge to the traditional canon of accepted knowledge (pp. 3-11). In other words, women and women's issues are a "breakout" or "topical" part of the curriculum study, becoming visible as a separate unit or separate study alongside the more traditional curriculum. This latter type of organization most clearly represents a multidisciplinary approach, or perhaps even an interdisciplinary one.

In her descriptions of Phase Four and Five curricula, we begin to see the striking overlap of these curricula types with interdisciplinary or, especially, the integrated curriculum. In Phase Four the question changed from "Did women write anything good?" to "What did women write?" (p. 17). Teaching materials become more non-traditional and, as a result of the use of new materials, the teacher is less likely to be viewed as an expert, and the boundaries between disciplines begin to blur. McIntosh is not sure Phase Five is operational yet; it is a curriculum reconstructed to be all inclusive of humankind, an imagined multicultural curriculum that includes, yet goes beyond, Phase 4, and that "fosters a pluralistic understanding and fulfills the dream of a common language" (p. 33). Although these latter two phases are not yet fully operational, Chapman (1997) outlines a vision of both Phases Four and Five, attempting to describe characteristics, questions, and learning assumptions that would underlie each curriculum type, and the advantages and problems of each (Chapman, 1997, pp. 48-53), especially as these relate to gender issues.

The AAUW publication *How Schools Shortchange Girls* (1992) grimly reports that schools tend to develop and teach a curriculum that reflects McIntosh's Phases One and Two (p. 65). Clearly, the road to an integrated curriculum, which resembles Phases Four and Five, will not be an easy one, even using Chapman's recent and helpful outlines. How might we imagine that these last two curriculum models, with their compatible systems of instruction, be developed for boys and girls in the middle school?

While none of the resources we are about to refer to really addresses gender issues per se, each of them rests upon a curricular vision grounded on democratic notions of schooling, and a belief that equity in education means assuming that both boys and girls can learn and achieve to each individual's full potential. While not all middle level curriculum theorists agree on how the ideal curriculum should look, James Beane (1993) speaks for all middle level curriculum integrationists when he says that the middle school curriculum should "respect the dignity of early adolescents . . . ," and that curriculum should "honor diversity" (pp. 18-19). In fact, he says "an enduring concept that ought to permeate the curriculum is that of . . . the related ideas of freedom, equality, caring, justice, and peace" (p. 66). We assume that the diversity he refers to implies gender, just as we assume that the democratic environment described for this level arises out of true collaboration and community, born of individuals who collectively respect and learn from one another.

For Beane, as well as for other theorists like Brazee and Capelluti (1995), the integrated curriculum is best characterized by thematic units with organizers extending from adolescent needs and larger community issues (Beane, 1993, p. 68). While Brazee and Capelluti's text *Dissolving Boundaries* (1995) and Stevenson and Carr's *Integrated Studies in the Middle Grades* (1993) do not offer specific gender-based study, their texts do describe actual efforts and curricular work based on the notions behind integrated curriculum. They are curricular conceptions that allow for conscious explorations of equity in human relations, and they break down old subject-centered and tradition-bound instruction, thus modeling more closely the visions McIntosh described in her Phases Four and Five. The increasing existence of such texts as these, is, of course, the reason why we said earlier in the chapter that middle school curricular thinking may be positioned to overtake a traditional curricular structure that is inherently gender-biased.

A Final Caveat:
The Textbook and the Gender-Fair Curriculum
We have alluded in various parts of the last two chapters to the importance of texts, while conceding that many are still not the gender-equitable materials they ought to be. Many professional groups and organizations have taken to heart these concerns and developed critical reading guidelines for educators who wish to select the most equitable texts available to promote gender-fair curriculum and instruction in their classes.

The Utah State Department of Education's gender equity training materials (1995) include a guide from GrayMill to help analyze texts and other materials for gender equity. The guide includes the following eight areas, which are printed on a rating scale so that each book or piece of material can be rated from good to poor on the gender criteria:

- avoids stereotypical portrayals
- portrays people in non-stereotyped roles
- avoids use of biased language
- includes examples of females' contributions
- includes information about females of all cultures
- pays attention to women's social issues
- balances social issues with political and military issues
- shows a wide variety of career options for men and women.

(Excerpted from Grayson, D. A., & Martin, M. D. (1997).
Generating expectations for student achievement. Canyon Lake, CA: GrayMill.)

If textual materials are found to fall short in representing both males' and females' issues or achievements, the Utah guide suggests supplementing the text readings with primary sources that do fill in the missing perspectives.

The good news may be that, as the AAUW report (1992) describes, virtually all textbook companies now have guides for nonsexist language; many, in fact, have stepped up their efforts to incorporate women's achievements and topics in the content of their books. Unfortunately, these guidelines are not always enforced. Still, teachers must make the best selections they can and supplement where they must, since research does indicate that books influence children's values about gender and multicultural issues, both positively and negatively (p. 62).

Cross-Disciplinary Methods for Gender-Equitable Instruction in Any Curriculum Framework

Much is written in the literature on multicultural (including gender) education and the positive effect of student-centered methods, such as cooperative learning and small group work in general, and the positive student and teacher collaboration possible within whole language environments. Increasingly, too, teachers find alternative assessments an attractive way to empower a diversity of students, because they permit students to show their strengths and learning in ways that match their learning styles.

While many of these methods are now widely accepted, educators are becoming increasingly aware of a darker side to these approaches. We do not mean to debunk these methods—we merely wish to point out the pitfalls. Such awareness is necessary if we are to carry them out well, with sensitivity.

The positive association of female and minority students' achievement with approaches such as cooperative and group learning, whole language environments, inquiry and problem-solving about real and important events, comes from a cross-section of literature: 1) studies on development and learning styles as they related to children, adolescents, and adults; 2) writings on successful strategies in the classroom in various fields such as language arts, the sciences, or mathematics; 3) multicultural education; and 4) women's studies. Doubtless, other sources are also available, but women's studies seems most pertinent to our study.

In the mid-1980s Belenky and her colleagues published *Women's Ways of Knowing* (1986), a book that challenged the male paradigms of intellectual development. They described various stages that women go through as they develop as knowers, thinkers, and learners in academics. They found the women they studied to be collaborative learners, who learned most when an experiential component was involved and when a classroom provided a "culture for growth" (p. 221). In essence, Belenky and her colleagues began to think of women as "connected" knowers, who learned best in collaboration with others, and when experience could be connected in some way with the material. Along with Carol Gilligan's work (1982) on women's moral development, which suggested that women follow a slightly different moral development path than men, and the learning style literature, which suggested that many females tended to be "relational" learners (Anderson & Adams, 1992), a rather general picture of females emerged as learners who often respond better to, and gain more success with, alternative paths of learning. While these initial studies were often done with females much older than young adolescents, experience, time, and more studies show similar preferences among younger females. The passages above may sound tentatively worded, and indeed they are, as none of these findings should be expected to characterize all females. Any general findings about a group should be

Alternative assessments are an attractive way to empower a diversity of students.

subordinate to information about the individual student, male or female.

In spite of that important caveat, educators have become more and more reliant on those methods that offer an advantage to learners who prefer collaboration, process-oriented work, hands-on inquiries that are based on real life, and, at best, connections between real life and more abstract knowledge, concepts, and theories. Many educators have determined that all children, regardless of gender, race, or national origin, can benefit from a learning environment structured to support these pedagogies, and from a concurrent curriculum. Again, as we shall see, these ideas need to be applied by someone conscious of possible hidden problems so that he or she can address those problems in the interest of an even more improved and equitable learning environment.

The Case For and Against Making Cooperative Learning Gender Fair

Theresa McCormick (1994) puts the case for cooperative learning about as clearly as anyone. Her thoughts describe all of our expectations of the pedagogy:

To restructure curriculum and instruction with structured and well-monitored cooperative learning methods would help redress the present imbalance and appeal more to the need for relationships and interconnections voiced by many students of color and female students. This is not to say that white male students will not benefit from cooperative learning activities. Ideally, they would benefit by having the opportunity to exercise their feminine traits . . . which, for the most part, are devalued by society. On the other hand, cooperative learning activities offer female students the opportunity to exercise their female "voice" and to integrate elements of the male "voice," such as decisiveness, leadership, and objectivity. (p. 65)

Then she drops the other shoe: "However, few schools operate under ideal conditions" (p. 65). Indeed, we know they do not, and they will not, which, of course, does not excuse educators from trying to do better. Numerous educators agree with McCormick's list of problems, which includes social dominance by males in the group and the dominance of male communication patterns or styles of speaking (p. 65).

Cohen (1994) also cites the problem of dominance and a resulting inequality in groups. Furthermore, Orenstein's observations of middle school teachers and girls, recounted in *SchoolGirls* (1994), yield a similar observance; that is, even teachers who used cooperative learning were becoming aware that, if unmonitored, the groups shored up student stereotypes, gender included (p. 30). The authors of *School Talk* (Eder, Evans, & Parker, 1995) are more vehement in describing the basic problem, finding that groups still allow for "aggressive competition" (p. 6).

While these are references to problems from general studies, specific subject studies also reverberate with the same problems. In her studies of peer-led discussion groups, Evans (1996a, 1996b) found that in these unsupervised groups, which were mixed-groups, boys dominated the conversations, wresting control from girls and guiding the conversation along the lines they wished to pursue. Girls' attempts to bring the conversation back to their themes or to the assignments met with little success. Evans (1996b) questioned the "assumption that such contexts are equitable places for students to assume ownership of their learning where all voices are heard and valued" (p. 201). Kahle and Meece (1994), in discussing findings on science instruction, also noted that:

some evidence suggests that cooperative learning may not be effective in increasing girls' participation and achievement in science. In mixed-sex small groups, girls are less likely to receive help from boys, and girls are less likely than boys to assume a leadership role. (p. 550)

What to do? We are all supposed to be on the cutting edge of the profession, implementing as many new techniques as possible to make our instruction more accessible for everyone. Yet we run quickly into problems. Should we abandon new techniques in favor of yesteryear's techniques? Not if we want to continue pursuing gender-equitable education. Instead, educators will do better to look to small-group learning and cooperative learning strategies.

The key words in the criticisms of such methods appear to be "unmonitored" or "unsupervised." It seems clear that the teacher must be aware of potential problems, be present in order to spot them, and make direct interventions where necessary. One of the teachers quoted by Orenstein says, "When they really act out, though, I'll just stop the class and wait . . ." (p. 31). Elizabeth Cohen (1994) developed perhaps even more effective strategies. She suggests:

- having different students play different roles over group assignments
- training students to be aware of these problems
- doing peer evaluations
- implementing groups in gradually ascending stages of difficulty, not sophisticated ones all at once
- preparing your environment for the use of groups
- using teacher intervention in appropriate ways.

Most helpful is her list of norms to be achieved:

- making sure everyone participates and helps
- giving everyone a part to play, and then rotating the parts
- making everyone's competence evident
- convincing the students that they all have multiple and different abilities
- breaking up tasks as abilities. (Cohen, 1994)

Cohen's entire book, *Designing Groupwork*, is sensitive and thoughtfully written, filled with helpful ideas for retrieving and enacting that ideal view of cooperative learning and small group learning as a pedagogy of equity. Before throwing up your hands and giving up on the idea of groups, read the book and find a powerful way to restructure and reteach boys and girls to interact well with each other in the middle level classroom.

Gender and Reading/Writing Workshop Approaches
In the same way as cooperative learning instruction, the reading and writing workshop classroom has become a desirable mode of classroom interaction for many teachers, whether they are working on teams or working alone with middle schoolers. Recent studies share insights that can help us improve the approach and, in doing so, help us make a classroom more equitable, not only with regard to gender, but also to socioeconomic class and cultural diversity. In mixed gender literature discussion groups, Evans (1996b) found that boys and girls could exercise power, or become disempowered, by what she called "positioning"—a place one inhabits in a conversation in relation to the others in the group, which is either self-enacted or imposed upon an individual group member by the others (p. 195). Within a framework using this concept, she found in her study of a 5th-grade classroom that the most obvious social marker for positioning was gender, and that a majority of marginalizing was done by boys of girls as speakers, but that girls could also marginalize a lone boy in a group conversation (p. 201).

Finders's study (1997) of hidden literacies uncovers differences among middle school girls themselves and the ways they perceive the "sanctioned literacies" (Finders defines this as the literacies sanctioned by adult educators) (p. 24), and the ways they use the "literature underlife" (p. 24) to create a space for themselves and their diverse needs. Finders's study suggested that many of the assumptions that underlie current student-centered reading and writing workshop pedagogy need to be re-examined. Calling the assumptions "myths of student-centered pedagogy," she outlines several areas teachers should re-examine in light of her study with groups of girls just entering a junior high: 1) the myth of the classroom as safe haven, 2) the myth that a safe classroom will create that comfort needed for taking learning risks, 3) the myth of a single classroom community that will be inclusive of all students, and 4) the myth that students have free choices for reading and writing that are free from their social relationships and social politics (pp. 118-121).

Finders learned from the groups of girls she studied that social and political contexts beyond the classroom directly influenced how these girls approached their classroom interactions and learning, and she feared that these assumptions or "myths" about student-centered pedagogy masked the influence of other lived contexts and roles (p. 118). Truly a breakthrough study, the work needs to be read in its entirety, because it does not suggest that we abandon pedagogies that focus on students nor that we return to traditional pedagogies, but rather that we begin to bring a critical "sociocultural perspective into the middle school classroom . . ." (p. 126).

Inquiry-oriented instruction has the potential for equitable outcomes.

In essence then, once again, making oneself aware of the complex issues that underlie our instruction and our classrooms, just as we must become aware of our own beliefs and assumptions about gender, is a necessary beginning to the wise use of instructional approaches. Also implied is that as part of the implementation of these pedagogies comes the necessary aim of creating a conversation in which students themselves become aware of these complexities and the effect of gender issues on their own learning. In writing about enlightening very young students to the gender issues in their own writing, McAuliffe (1993-94) suggested that a great deal of time for conferencing might help students go beyond their own unconscious "genderlects"—as long as that conferencing also focused on helping students see their own styles as gender-based and pushed them to explore story styles generally characterizing the opposite gender. In other words, a process writing pedagogy could work, with directed effort, to address other complex issues and learnings. In a similar vein, Finders (1997), arguing for a better, more critically aware use of student-centered pedagogies, advocated "sociocultural pedagogy," one that "provides students with the tools necessary to examine the powerful constraints that serve to define them" (p. 127). The openness of workshops for reading and writing cannot in itself guarantee that important issues (about gender and other topics) influencing learning will be addressed; teachers must use this open atmosphere to open up even further the major issues affecting young adolescents.

Problem-Solving and Inquiry As Learning Strategies for Both Genders

To help address the dearth of women in mathematics and science fields, educators have begun focusing on the approaches of problem-solving and inquiry as they relate to gender. Recent studies acknowledge that in the past, males tended to be found superior in their word problem-solving abilities. At least one recent study (Zambo & Follman, 1993), however, found that girls may have a slight edge in this area when articulated steps in a plan are overtly used. In other words, "a step-by-step approach to solving word problems might assist in reducing the gender gap in problem-solving ability" (p. 8). Likewise, Allen (1995) found that teachers can help develop girls' confidence in math and science by thoroughly teaching problem-solving processes. Kreinberg (1989) noted that "mathematics classrooms where equity is a priority are characterized by an emphasis on problem solving . . ." (p. 130). In the science field, Kahle (1990) noted that inquiry-oriented instruction has the potential of producing equitable outcomes in attitude and achievement. Another study (Shepardson & Pizzini, 1994), done with 7th-and 8th-grade students, also gives evidence that inquiry-oriented instruction has the potential for equitable outcomes (p. 192).

Mathematics and the sciences are not the only fields where problem-solving and inquiry-oriented instruction has been suggested for use. Social studies educators have promoted this approach to instruction by advocating the study of problems and themes, ones that could be demystified for learners through relevant student investigations and discussion. Furthermore, the spirit of problem-solving and inquiry permeates the best literature explorations, with profound questions becoming the impetus for an exploration of issues focusing on characters, themes, and social connections with fiction, as well as the periods in which the writers lived and developed their art.

Thus, inquiry and problem-solving do not belong to the sciences and mathematics alone, but are at the core of much important learning; indeed, they really may be at the heart of all learning as the means by which we can follow our curiosity toward finding our own answers about life and its challenges. Certainly, inquiry and problem-solving are at the center of the interdisciplinary unit and the integrated curriculum—those curriculum structures that we find highly supportive of gender equitable learning.

The more interdisciplinary or integrated the curriculum becomes, the more opportunity there is, and the more necessity, for inquiry approaches, and group or individual investigations. A few good sources bring this point home. While not focused specifically on gender issues, the following texts do at least focus on middle level students as inquirers. Stevenson's *Teachers As Inquirers: Strategies for Learning with and About Early Adolescents* (1986) is an older text, yet it is not dated. Stevenson not only explores the concept of inquiry, but also offers suggestions for guiding, implementing, and assessing inquiry instruction. Martinello's and Cook's (1994) book *Interdisciplinary Inquiry in Teaching and Learning* explores the nature of, and history behind, inquiry, moving into ideas for constructing an interdisciplinary curriculum to promote all students' problem-solving abilities. Finally, interested readers should check out Ross Burkhardt's *The Inquiry Process: Student-Centered Learning* (1994), which offers classroom-tested approaches to authentic inquiries and assessments within interdisciplinary problem-centered units.

Gender and Authentic or Alternative Assessments

It seems clear to most educators that implementing an authentic pedagogy inside any curricular framework (authentic pedagogy, according to Newman, Marks, and Gamoran [1995], is daily teaching practices and assessments consistent with active learning, and connected to meaningful tasks that demand high intellectual quality) requires complex assessment of student learning. Performances, portfolios of various work, observations, interviews, videos, written works, or exhibitions of significant and worthwhile accomplished work allow both boys and girls to show their various achievements, each bearing their unique stamps. Alternative assessments go far beyond the world of the quiz and the test, and honor the individual strengths of both boys and girls as they demonstrate accomplishments inside frameworks of curriculum and instruction. As Kreinberg (1989) says in relation to mathematics and alternative assessment, "As long as tests drive the curriculum, and teachers are pressured to teach to the tests, we will not have a mathematics curriculum that is rich and flexible enough to provide access for all students" (p. 141). McCormick (1994) adds: "Many types of assessment strategies are necessary to evaluate students' achievement and progress in a non-sexist . . . manner" (p. 132).

Newman, Marks, and Gamoran (1995) offer more evidence that authentic assessment tasks, along with appropriate pedagogy practices, serve the cause of equitable education. Their study found that, "Regardless of race or gender, an average student would move from the 30th to the 60th percentile if he or she received high authentic pedagogy . . . " (p. 7). They continue, "While disparities between different groups remain, using the standards to evaluate the quality of pedagogy and student performance creates no additional roadblocks to the important work of closing those performance gaps" (p. 8). Ultimately, they agreed with Kreinberg (1989), who noted that "authentic pedagogy helps all students substantially" (p. 8). Educators studying assessments have focused keenly in recent years on the potential effect of assessments on students' diversity. Gordon (1992) noted that to be equitable, assessments should provide, among other things: task content with contexts, diversity, flexibility in timing, self-selected options, and use of both individual and cooperative performance opportunities. Many other suggestions for authentic assessments exemplify these characteristics. (A particularly helpful text is Herbert Grossman's *Teaching in a Diverse Society* (1995), a preservice methods book that includes several chapters on the appropriate selection of assessment strategies.)

In the chart on the next page, we identify the type of assessment that may generally correspond to the type of curriculum framework used. While there is no particular reason why curriculum and instruction planned from a traditional standpoint cannot revolve around authentic pedagogies and assessments, the truth is that they often do not. If concerns for gender equity are considered, however, then the assessments and strategies would more resemble the kinds of assessments frequently used in interdisciplinary and integrated curriculum models.

Typical Ways of Assessing Students and Units of Study

Traditional Subject-centered

Students: traditional student tests at the end of the study
Teacher: teacher's informal notes on plans

Multidisciplinary Curriculum and Instruction

Students: traditional student tests, papers, some projects
Teacher: have students informally evaluate how they liked the unit

Interdisciplinary Units of Study

Students: projects and performances usually provide ways to assess application of knowledge and skills, a rating scale or other instrument needed
                could use traditional means (tests with open-ended items)
Teacher: team log of daily meetings
                individual team member keeps the journal of impressions and shares with team
                student final is reflective response papers on unit

Integrated Curriculum and Instruction

Students: self assessment, journals, conferences
                peer evaluation of efforts
                little traditional assessment
Teacher: weekly evaluations (team, and self)
                reflective journals
                daily observations of student plans and reports
                weekly conferences and anecdotal records
                team or individual teaching log

Gender-Based Classes: Yes or No?

In the last few years, purposefully segregating groups of similar students whom educators perceive to be at-risk has emerged as a popular strategy. By separating out types of students, giving them challenging instruction, offering teachers who are caring and energetic role models, and pushing them, educators often see improvements in these students who, they believe, otherwise would have become lost in the system. Several schools have become sites for educating only African American boys, for example, an idea that has been challenged in the courts. Other plans have pinpointed not whole schools for perceived at-risk groups of learners, but classes of segregated groups within their schools. Many of these plans target gender as a risk-forming variable, especially since the publication of AAUW's *How Schools Shortchange Girls* (1992), and they develop programs for girls-only classes, particularly in science and math.

While it is still too early to determine if the idea works well in all cases and circumstances, it nevertheless has led to arguments as to whether it is best to segregate girls from boys in classes. Palar (1996) described one school in West Des Moines, Iowa, that tried single-gender, 4th-grade classes for one class a day, separating girls from boys in mathematics classes (p. 38). The teachers reported gaining an increased awareness of their own behaviors, noting that they did, indeed, sometimes respond more to outspoken boys, thus leaving out the more silent girls. The teachers realized that this behavior often put more stress on boys by expecting too much from them, while they did not hold the same exacting expectations for girls (pp. 40-41).

Teachers often put more stress on boys by expecting too much from them.

Perry (1996) reported trying gender-grouped classes in a grade 6-8 school in Virginia. As principal, he made his staff aware of gender issues and bias; consequently, the teachers suggested trying gender-grouped classes for two out of seven periods a day in math and science as an experiment. Enrollment in these classes was voluntary; if a student preferred being in a co-educational class, he or she was placed in one (pp. 32-33). While it is too early to determine how the experiment affected students' achievement, observations made by students, parents, and teachers indicated that the experiment was worth pursuing. Pollina (1995), writing about the lessons private, all-girls schools can teach us about appropriate classroom environments and pedagogy, described another experiment used in single-gender classrooms at the Illinois Mathematics and Science Academy in Aurora. Although this experiment focused on high school learners, the information is enlightening. The school offered an all-girls section on mechanics as part of a calculus-based physics course (p. 32). The results a year later: "Girls performed on par with their male peers; . . . more girls enrolled in and successfully completed the year-long physics course than ever before; and girls in the single-gender section gained more self-confidence than did those in co-educational sections" (p. 33).

However much this strategy might sound like a panacea, educators have weighed the positives with the cautions coming out of this literature. The positives seem to be:

- Teachers may be more likely to critically examine their own hidden biases and gendered-teaching behaviors (Palar, 1996, pp. 40-41).
- Girls in particular do seem to benefit from increased self-esteem and confidence, particularly in science and math, and seem to be able to learn more readily in an environment in which their learning styles can dominate (Pollina, 1995, p. 33).
- Perry (1996) and teachers at his school observed that:
  - girls felt freer to speak out in same-gender classes
  - grade point averages for both genders were higher in same-sex classes
  - there were fewer discipline problems reported in gender-grouped sections
  - boys expressed relief that they did not have to impress girls (pp. 33-34).

Important reasons also exist, however, for keeping boys and girls together, while trying to remain gender equitable:

- Boys may need the feminine perspective in their classes to help control or monitor their behaviors (Palar, 1996).
- Boys may actually learn more with girls present, since girls tend to ask more questions and slow down the pace of the class (Palar, 1996).
- Gender-grouped classes might send messages to females that the reasons for separation extend from their inability to compete in a "real mathematics or science classroom" (Pollina, 1995, p. 32); such a message could do far more harm to female learners than most co-educational environments.

The biggest reason why educators may need to abandon the idea of the single-gender classroom may be the legal issues associated with segregating the sexes. Most public schools may not be able to enact rules allowing the formation of these classrooms (while private schools are not governed by such laws). Nonetheless, some believe that co-educational environments can profit from the lessons being learned in single-gender environments. It is not just a legal issue. For many, it is a philosophical one—a belief that boys and girls must learn to work together respectfully in order to become adults who can do so.

Can co-educational environments be more gender-fair? Even those who have taught in single-gender settings have some ideas. For example, consider the following:

- The teacher profiled by Pollina at the Illinois Mathematics and Science Academy in Aurora (1995) regrouped his classes into co-educational ones. Upon finding that boys' responses tended to dominate again, he had everyone write down questions to answers rather than speak them, a strategy that made the environment more equitable again (p. 33).
- Many educators have found certain strategies to be generally helpful to

girls' learning (but not detrimental to boys'), including collaborative processes, hands-on experimentation, and connecting abstract concepts to concrete realities (p. 32).

- From a larger programmatic view, Palar (1996) points to the New Jersey program called STAGE, in which students and teachers are taught about gender differences. Students from various schools attend workshops, then return to teach others about gender issues and equity. The heightened awareness of the harmful effects of gender bias is evident in both boys' and girls' comments about appropriate and inappropriate comments, language, and behaviors (p. 42).

Readers need to remember that most of the suggestions in this section deal with science and mathematics classes, and come from a relatively small, but representative sample of similar recent experiments with same-sex classes. Are gender-based classes appropriate? There are pros and cons. Knowing them and proceeding carefully, with an eye to the impact of gender on all students' education is the only surety right now.

What Teachers Can Do Now in Their Classrooms

Chapter 3 reviewed the strategies that educators, parents, and concerned individuals could use to promote gender-equitable environments in school. The reality is that most teachers spend most of their days in their own classrooms, or in the classrooms of their teammates, as they work together with students or on team matters. Given the amount of literature on this subject, teachers could find suggestions for any discipline, whether it be health, physical education, mathematics, or English/language arts and reading. In addition, many general things can be done to help maintain a gender-fair environment in the classroom:

- Take one of the self-introspective surveys dealing with gender bias, and be as honest with yourself as you can.
- Try to videotape a class and watch it with a specific focus on obvious, unconscious, or potential bias areas that you see (Bellamy, 1994). Watch for your own use of sexist language and behaviors, and watch for your own interaction patterns. Are you consistently favoring one gender over the other? Overhelping girls? Asking either gender different levels of questions?
- Look carefully at your room's physical aspects. Are visual materials representative of girls or women, as well as boys or men? Are the girls or women portrayed in powerful roles? Are the written texts that accompany the visuals free of sexist language?
- Watch for equitable exchanges among students in your classes. Change seating patterns from time to time so that different gender mixes are possible. Watch for gender patterns in group work.
- Research your own curriculum areas and incorporate the latest informa-

tion relating to gender. Check it for balance as much as you can. Think about how to do a Level Four or Five curriculum (McIntosh, 1983). Discuss with your team how to increase interdisciplinary work. Make sure your materials are gender-fair; specifically, ensure that they show females in strong roles and in typically male-oriented careers. Use supplementary outside materials if school texts do not seem gender equitable. And do not forget about appropriate assessments; allow for alternatives, so that boys and girls can all share their learning in a variety of appropriate ways.

- Invite both women and men role models to your classes. Use the community. The work done by the mothers may be nonstereotypical, and most mothers are happy to come to their child's school to talk about their careers (in spite of the fact that their middle schooler may shudder!)

- Create instructional opportunities for discussions of gender issues related to the topic of study. Make gender—the differences and similarities, and their implications for everyone—very visible in your classroom. Encourage students to learn about the other gender and to respect differences and look for our common humanity.

- Do classroom "action research" on gender (AAUW, 1996). Classroom inquiries can spark discussion among the team, or be a source for conversations.

Gender Fairness and the Middle School Concept: An Ecological Balance

We have made various linkages between the middle school concept and gender equitable-education. The authors believe that the middle school concept, and its various curricular and instructional components, undergirds and strongly supports gender-equitable education for young adolescents. Middle school educators know, however, that implementation of a middle school concept means implementing all of it—not just an advisory period, not just exploratories outside a core curriculum, not just interdisciplinary team organization, and not just common team planning. All of these components must be instituted and harmoniously balanced if a healthy middle school environment is to thrive and give life to all who inhabit it.

In the same way, educators, parents, the community and, of course, the students themselves cannot expect that a truly gender-equitable education will be promoted if only some classes deal with gender issues, or if only some teachers do. As Anne Chapman says, "Education is a seamless web. What happens in one subject's class affects what happens in another class . . ." (Acher, 1997). The authors of *Growing Smart* (AAUW, 1995) clearly make the case for nothing short of a systemic change in education: ". . . gender equity is still a long way from being realized, and, on the front lines of the battle, teachers have learned they can accomplish more when the rest of the community fights alongside them" (p. iv). They state clearly that the ecological, systemic kind of thinking is necessary because simply "tinkering at the edges of our educational structure" (p. iv) just will not accomplish for all kids what we need to accomplish.

References

Acher, J. (1997, March 5). Gender studies helping both girls and boys, book argues. *Education Week, 16*, pp. 14+.

Allen, D. (1995). Encouraging success in female students: Helping girls develop math and science skills. *Gifted Child Today Magazine, 18*, 44-45.

American Association of University Women. (1992). *How schools shortchange girls.* Washington, DC: Author.

American Association of University Women. (1995). *Growing smart: What's working for girls in school.* Washington, DC: Author.

American Association of University Women. (1996). *Girls in the middle: Working to succeed in school.* Washington, DC: Author.

Anderson, J., & Adams, M. (1992). Acknowledging the learning styles of diverse student populations: Implications for instructional design. In L. Border & N. Chism (Eds.), *Teaching for diversity* (pp. 19-33). San Francisco: Jossey-Bass Publishers.

Beane, J. (1993). *A middle school curriculum: From rhetoric to reality* (2nd ed.). Columbus, OH: National Middle School Association.

Belenky, M., Cinchy, B., Goldberger, N., & Tarule, J. (1986). *Women's ways of knowing: The development of self, voice, and mind.* New York: Basic Books.

Bellamy, N. (1994). Bias in the classroom: Are we guilty? *Science Scope, 6*, 60-63.

Blum-Anderson, J. (1989, November). *Affect and mathematics: Persistence in the mathematics environment.* Paper presented at the Conference on Women and Mathematics, St. Cloud, MN.

Brazee, E., & Capelluti, J. (1995). *Dissolving boundaries: Toward an integrated curriculum.* Columbus, OH: National Middle School Association.

Burkhardt, R. (1994). *The inquiry process: Student centered learning.* Logan, IA: Perfection Learning.

Butler, D., & Sperry, S. (1991). Gender issues and the middle school curriculum. *Middle School Journal, 23*(2), 18-23.

Cai, J. (1995, October). *Exploring gender differences in solving open-ended mathematical problems.* Paper presented at North American Chapter of the International Group for the Psychology of Mathematics Education, Columbus, OH.

Campbell, P. (1992). *Nothing can stop us now: Designing effective programs for girls in math, science, and engineering* [Brochure]. Newton, MA: WEEA Publishing Center.

Carlson, M. (1989). Guidelines for a gender-balanced curriculum in English, grades 7-12. *English Journal, 78*, 30-33.

Chapman, A. (1997). *A great balancing act: Equitable education for girls and boys.* Washington, DC: National Association of Independent Schools.

Cherland, M. (1992). Gendered readings: Cultural restraints upon response to literature. *The New Advocate, 5*, 187-198.

Christian-Smith, L. (1993). Voices of resistance: Young women readers of romance fiction. In L. Weis & M. Fine (Eds.), *Beyond silenced voices* (pp. 169-189). New York: SUNY Press.

Cohen, E. (1994). *Designing groupwork: Strategies for the heterogeneous classroom* (2nd ed.). New York: Teachers College Press.

Connecticut State Board of Education. (1995). *A guide to curriculum development in family and consumer sciences education.* Hartford, CT: Author.

Davies, B. (1989). The discursive production of the male/female dualism in school settings. *Oxford Review of Education, 15,* 229-241.

Eder, D., Evans, C., & Parker, S. (1995). *School talk: Gender and adolescent culture.* New Brunswick, NJ: Rutgers University Press.

Evans, K. (1996a). A closer look at literature discussion groups: The influence of gender on student response and discourse. *The New Advocate, 9,* 183-197.

Evans, K. (1996b). Creating spaces for equity? The role of positioning in peer-led literature discussions. *Language Arts, 73,* 194-202.

Finders, M. (1997). *Just girls: Hidden literacies and life in junior high.* Urbana, IL: National Council of Teachers of English.

Gilligan, C. (1982). *In a different voice: Psychological theory and women's development.* Cambridge, MA: Harvard University Press.

Gordon, E. (1992). *Implications of diversity in human characteristics for authentic assessment. Position paper.* Los Angeles, CA: Center for Research on Evaluation, Standards, and Student Testing.

Gray-Schlegel, M., & Gray-Schlegel, T. (1995-1996). An investigation of gender stereotypes as revealed through children's creative writing. *Reading Research and Instruction, 35,* 160-170.

Grayson, D. A., & Martin, M. D. (1997). *Generating expectations for student achievement.* Canyon Lake, CA: GrayMill.

Greely, M. P. (1992). Finding the answers: A women's history bee. *The Book Report, 10,* 30.

Grossman, H. (1995). *Teaching in a diverse society.* Needham Heights, MA: Allyn and Bacon.

Jacobs, H. H. (1989). *Interdisciplinary curriculum: Design and implementation.* Alexandria, VA: Association of Supervision and Curriculum Development.

Jensen, R., & McMullen, D. (1995, April). *A study of gender differences in the math and science career interests of gifted fifth and sixth graders.* Paper presented at the American Educational Research Association, New Orleans, LA.

Kahle, J. (1990). Why girls don't know. In M. Rowe (Ed.), *What research says to the science teacher. Vol. 6* (pp. 55-67). Washington, DC: National Science Teachers Association.

Kahle, J., & Meece, J. (1994). Research on gender issues in the classroom. In D. Gabel (Ed.), *Handbook of research on science teaching and learning* (pp. 542-557). New York: McMillan.

Kreinberg, N. (1989). The practice of equity. *Peabody Journal of Education, 66,* 127-146.

Leder, G. (1992). Mathematics and gender: Changing perspectives. In D. Grouws (Ed.), *Handbook of research on mathematics teaching and learning* (pp. 597-622). New York: Macmillan.

Lirgg, C. (1993). Effects of same-sex versus coeducational physical education on the self-perceptions of middle and high school students. *Research Quarterly for Exercise and Sport, 64,* 324-334.

McIntosh, P. (1983). *Interactive phases of curricular revision: A feminist perspective.* (Working Paper No. 124). Wellesley, MA: Wellesley College, Center for Research on Women.

Martinello, M., & Cook, G. (1994). *Interdisciplinary inquiry in teaching and learning.* New York: Macmillan College Publishing.

McAuliffe, S. (1993-94). Toward understanding one another: Second graders' use of gendered language story styles. *The Reading Teacher, 41,* 302-310.

McCormick, T. (1994). *Creating the non-sexist classroom: A multicultural approach.* New York: Teachers College Press.

Newmann, F., Marks, H., & Gamoran, A. (1995). *Authentic pedagogy: Standards that boost student performance.* (Issue Report No. 8). Madison, WI: University of Wisconsin, Madison, Center for Educational Research.

Orenstein, E. (1994). *Schoolgirls: Young women, self-esteem, and the confidence gap.* New York: Doubleday.

Palar, B. (1996, October). A study in contrasts. *Better Homes and Gardens, 74,* 38, 40-43.

Perry, W. (1996, February). Gender-based education: Why it works at the middle school level. *NASSP Bulletin, 80,* 32-35.

Pollina, A. (1995). Gender balance: Lessons from girls in science and mathematics. *Educational Leadership, 53,* 30-34.

Rand, D., & Gibb, L. (1989). A model program for gifted girls in science. *Journal for the Education of the Gifted, 12,* 142-155.

Restructuring education: Getting girls into America's goals. (1990). *Outlook, 84,* 1-6.

Sells, L. W. (1980). The mathematics filter and the education of women and minorities. In L. Fox, C. Brady, & K. Tobin (Eds.), *Women and the mathematic mystique* (pp. 66-75). Baltimore, MD: Johns Hopkins University Press.

Shakeshaft, C., Gilligan, C., & Pierce, D. (1986). A gender at risk. *Phi Delta Kappan, 67,* 499-503.

Shepardson, D., & Pizzini, E. (1994). Gender, achievement, and perception toward science activities. *School Science and Mathematics, 94,* 188-193.

Shmurak, C., & Ratliff, J. (1994). Gender equity and gender bias: Issues for the middle school teacher. *Middle School Journal, 25,* 63-66.

Sprouse, J., & Webb, J. (1994). *The Pygmalian effect and its influence on the grading and gender assignment on spelling and essay assignments.* Unpublished masters thesis, University of Virginia, Charlottesville, VA.

Stevenson, C. (1986). *Teachers as inquirers: Strategies for learning with and about early adolescents.* Columbus, OH: National Middle School Association.

Stevenson, C., & Carr, J. (1993). *Integrated studies in the middle grades: "Dancing through walls."* New York: Teachers College Press.

Twarek, L., & George, H. (1994). *Gender differences during recess in elementary schools.* Report from Danbury, OH, and Perkins, OH. (ERIC Document Reproduction Series No. ED 381277)

Utah State Department of Education. (1995). *MECCA: Making equity count for classroom achievement.* Salt Lake City, UT: Author.

Voorhees, J. (1994). *Promoting gender fairness in school curricula and classroom instruction through infusion of equitable resources, vocational programs, and staff development.* (ERIC Document Reproduction Service No. ED 389633)

Zambo, R., & Follman, J. (1993, April). *Gender-related differences in problem-solving at the 6th and 8th grade levels.* Paper presented at the American Educational Research Association, Atlanta, GA.

Part Three:
Gender, Young Adolescents, and Resources

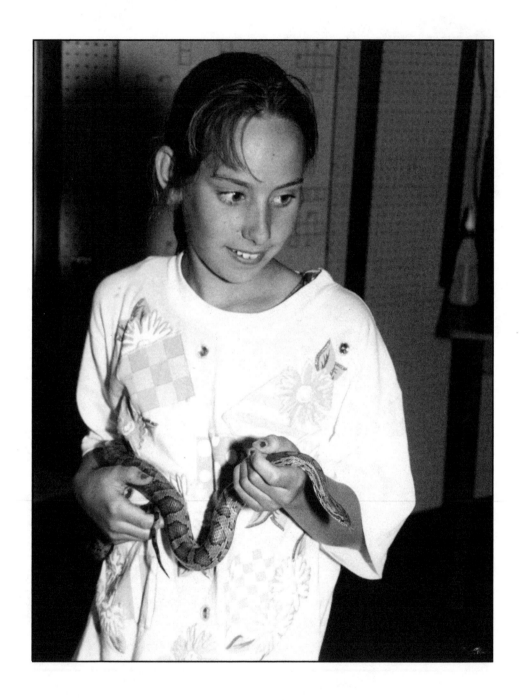

Chapter 5

Additional Sources
of Information

*F*ortunately, the research on gender differences and the call for gender-equitable and -responsive education experiences have resulted in more, and improved, resources. Now, educators have access to excellent print and audiovisual materials dealing with all aspects of education equity. This final chapter includes a list of selected annotated publications that call attention to the need for gender equity, and provide directions for gender-responsive educational experiences. We also offer a look at sources of additional information, such as organizations and associations promoting equity, professional associations, specific subject area associations, state departments of education, national resource centers, and youth organizations.

Resources from WEEA for Adults

The Women's Educational Equity Act (WEEA) is a federal mandate to promote educational equity for girls and women. Its objectives are: 1) to promote gender equity in education in the United States; 2) to promote equity in education for women and girls who suffer from multiple forms of discrimination based on sex, race, ethnic origin, limited-English proficiency, disability, or age; and 3) help educational agencies and institutions meet the requirements of Title IX of the Education Amendments of 1972. *Women's Educational Equity Act (WEEA), Education Development Center, 55 Chapel Hill Street, C-C97, Newton, MA 02158-1060, 412-741-1968; or www.edc.org/Women'sEquity*

Exploring Work: Fun Activities for Girls (1996).
This book helps girls explore a broad range of careers. *Exploring Work* is a fun, hands-on workbook containing 30 engaging activities. It addresses gender-role stereotyping and gender bias, and also provides suggestions about how to overcome them. Teachers, parents, counselors, and program coordinators will find this an invaluable career awareness resource and career exploration tool to be used any day of the year, at home or in school. These activities will give many students a glimpse of career possibilities they never before imagined.

Gender, Discourse, and Technology, by Katherine Henson (1997).
Technology has been a key force for change during this century, affecting every aspect of our professional and personal lives. Technology use and occupations are hailed as the new frontiers. How gender affects the application of this technology is an open question. *Gender, Discourse, and Technology* explores the perception that technology has a "male" persona, relates this discussion to the use of technology in classrooms, and examines the implications for the world of work.

Gender Equity for Educators, Parents, and Community (1995).
K-12 teachers, administrators, parents, and community programs will find that this book challenges those who have low expectations for either girls or boys. This booklet illustrates gender stereotyping and its relationship to students' success, helps readers explore new options, explains Title IX and how it supports equitable education, teaches how to recognize and respond to gender bias, and provides gender equity awareness exercises for teachers.

Lifting the Barriers: 600 Strategies That Really Work To Increase Girls' Participation in Science, Mathematics, and Computers, by Jo Sanders (1994).
Teachers found that using these strategies caused dramatic changes. Girls' enrollment in advanced courses and after-school clubs doubled or even tripled in one year. In one school, girls signed up for physics courses for the first time in 12 years.

Math and Science for the Co-ed Classroom (1996).
This is a useful pamphlet for math and science educators, administrators, counselors, parents, and community programs. It asks, "How do we ensure that all students—girls and boys—are engaged learners in math and science classes?" This informative pamphlet set, from a national expert in the field of equity in mathematics, science, and engineering, offers practical information that will help in assessing the school and classroom climate and in creating change.

New Moon Network: For Adults Who Care About Girls (New Moon Publishing, 1997).
This publication is for parents, educators, coaches, counselors, community program leaders, and anyone else working with girls. This monthly publication contains current research and effective methods for raising and supporting healthy, confident girls. Also, it offers readers an opportunity to share experiences, questions, and strategies with other concerned adults.

Women's Journeys, Women's Stories: In Search of Our Multicultural Future (1997).
This women's history curriculum complements the WEEA set *In Search of Our Past: Units in American History,* picking up where other history texts leave off, and updating previous historical accounts. *Women's Journeys, Women's Stories* presents a contemporary multicultural view, telling stories that fill critical gaps in the history of the United States.

Resources from WEEA for Students

Aruna's Journeys, 1997 (for girls ages 8-12).
Aruna's Journeys by Jyotana Sreenivasan (from the Smooth Stone Press and available through WEEA) is about Aruna's travels to India, and her journey to find her own self. This is the second look at girlhood and cultural issues by this talented author. This excellent discussion-starter includes a study guide for teachers.

The Moon Over Crete, 1996 (for girls 8-12).
The Moon Over Crete by Jyotana Sreenivasan (from the Smooth Stone Press and available through WEEA) is a story about 11-year-old Lily's journey back in time to a world of equity. With the help of her flute teacher, she travels to the Crete of 3,500 years ago to discover a civilization with gender equality.

New Moon: The Magazine for Girls and Their Dreams, 1997 (for girls ages 8-14).
This imaginative publication is created by and for girls. Professionally produced, *New Moon* is an advertisement-free international magazine that features stories by and about girls and women from all over the world. *New Moon* celebrates girls, explores the passage from girlhood to womanhood, and builds a healthy resistance to gender inequities.

WEEA Materials That Support Title IX Mandates

A-Gay-Yah: A Gender Equity Curriculum for Grades 6-12, 1992.
This multicultural curriculum emphasizes critical thinking and cooperative learning. *A-Gay-Yah* affirms Native Americans' long and vital cultural history, while helping students discuss gender issues related to traditional and modern culture. This curriculum complements social studies and history classrooms.

Equity in Education Series, 1995.
Various approaches are offered to meet the needs of all students in today's diverse classrooms. The series helps educators, parents, and community members understand their crucial roles in furthering equity in the schools and in society. It also helps users identify bias and respond with activities and hands-on tools.

Equity Lessons Series, 1982.
This innovative urban program was designed to develop an awareness of gender-role stereotyping. *Equity Lessons for Elementary School* can supplement any social studies curriculum. Its activities help students identify gender-role stereotyping on toy packaging, in advertising, and in fairy tales. *Equity Lessons for Secondary School* presents activities based on personal assumptions and meaning in the lives of women activists.

Gender Equity for Educators, Parents, and Community (La Igualdad de Género para Educadores, Padres, y la Comunidad), 1995.
This booklet will help educators to recognize the limits of assumptions based on gender, and it offers new options to teachers, parents, and community organizations. Now offered in English and Spanish, this best-selling booklet will soon be available in Vietnamese.

Going Places: An Enrichment Program To Empower Students, 1991.
Based on a project conducted in the San Diego City Schools, this program targets middle school students who are most at risk for dropping out. It focuses on enrichment and hands-on, cooperative group learning. Goals of the publication include developing and building self-esteem, improving problem-solving and decision-making skills, and developing leadership skills.

Just What the Doctor Should Have Ordered: A Prescription for Sex-Fair School Health Services, 1991.
This publication offers the first civil rights view of sex discrimination in health services. It includes an easy, step-by-step method for evaluating student health services. This vital guide clearly defines the legal responsibilities as required by Title IX, and helps schools negotiate ethical dilemmas.

Legislation for Change: A Case Study of Title IX and the Women's Educational Equity Act Program.
This working paper uses Title IX of the Education Amendments of 1972 as a case study to explore the education field and the effects of civil rights legislation dealing with gender. It discusses the origins and context of Title IX, and examines some of its successes and failures, closing with some points to consider when legislating for equity.

General Print Resources

The Beauty Myth: How Images of Beauty Are Used Against Women, by Naomi Wolf (William Morrow Publishing, 1991).
This publication examines how advertising creates an unattainable ideal of beauty.

Enlightened Racism: The Cosby Show, Audiences and the Myth of the American Dream, by Sut Jhally and Justin Lewis (Westview Press, 1992).
Media critics examine how the popular TV show influenced perceptions of race.

Media-tions: Forays into the Culture and Gender Wars, by Elayne Rapping (South End Press, 1994).
This collection of essays looks at how far women have come in the media—and how far they have yet to go.

Reading National Geographic, by Catherine A. Lutz and Jane L. Collins (University of Chicago Press, 1993).
This publication extends beyond the photography of *National Geographic* to critique the lauded magazine's editorial and photographic policies concerning race, class, gender, and ethnicity. This book turns a readily accessible classroom resource into a powerful teaching tool.

Where the Girls Are, by Susan J. Douglas (Times Books, 1994).
Where the Girls Are looks back at television programs, pop music, and advertisements over four decades to reveal the mixed messages conveyed to girls coming of age in America.

Organizations and Associations Promoting Equity

American Association of University Women (AAUW), 1111 Sixteenth Street, Washington, DC 20035-4873; 202-728-7602.
The AAUW provides a wealth of excellent publications that call attention to and promote gender equity, including:

> *AAUW Issue Briefs* (1990-1995). This set of five briefs explores gender equity issues, including treatment of students, educator training, the curriculum, college admissions testing, and education and training.

> *Girls Can! Community Coalitions Resource Manual* (1996). This comprehensive guide will help those organizations and individuals seeking to launch and sustain community-based programs for girls. It offers tips for building coalitions, recruiting volunteers, planning projects, raising funds, and gaining media attention. It also includes contact information for more than 200 national and grassroots organizations.

> *Girls in the Middle: Working To Succeed in School* (1996). This is a study of middle school girls and the strategies they use to meet the challenges of adolescence. The report links girls' success to school reforms, such as team teaching and cooperative learning, especially when they are used to address gender issues.

> *Girls in the Middle: Working To Succeed in School Video* (1996). This video offers an absorbing look at the strategies that girls in three middle schools use to meet challenges in their daily lives. A video guide with discussion questions, program resources, and action strategies is also included.

Growing Smart: What's Working for Girls in School Executive Summary and Action Guide (1995). This illustrated summary of an academic report identifies themes and approaches that promote girls' achievement and healthy development. Based on a review of more than 500 studies and reports, it includes action strategies, a program resource list, and firsthand accounts of some program participants.

Hostile Hallways: The AAUW Survey on Sexual Harassment in America's Schools (1993). Based on the experiences of 1,632 students in grades 8-11, this is the first national study of sexual harassment in school. The report includes gender and ethnic/racial data breakdowns.

How Schools Shortchange Girls: The AAUW Report. (Marlowe paperback edition, 1995.) This publication shows how girls are disadvantaged in America's schools and includes recommendations for educators and policymakers, as well as concrete strategies for change.

SchoolGirls: Young Women, Self-Esteem, and the Confidence Gap. (Doubleday, 1994.) This riveting book by journalist Peggy Orenstein, in association with AAUW, shows how girls in two racially and economically diverse California communities suffer a painful plunge in self-esteem.

Shortchanging Girls, Shortchanging America Executive Summary (1994). This is a summary of the 1991 poll that assessed the self-esteem, educational experiences, and career aspirations of girls and boys, ages 9-15. This revised edition reviews the poll's impact, offers action strategies, and highlights survey results with charts and graphs.

Shortchanging Girls, Shortchanging America Video (1991). This dramatic look at the inequities girls face in school features education experts and public policy leaders, AAUW poll results, and the compelling voices and faces of American girls.

Brave Girls and Strong Women Bookstore, http://members.aol.com.brvgirls.
The Brave Girls and Strong Women Bookstore, on the World Wide Web, offers over 40 empowering books for young people, all from small publishers dedicated to creating a world of equality. There is also a list of books about what parents and teachers can do to address girls' loss of self-esteem. Interviews with authors of empowering books for girls provide more insight into their books and their inspirations. This site also includes a list of links to other Web sites that can help girls take charge of their lives and the world. A six-page Brave Girls and Strong Women book list can be obtained by writing: Jyotsna Sreenivasan, P.O. Box 15481, Washington, DC 20003-0481.

EQUALS, Lawrence Hall of Science, University of California, Berkeley CA 94702-5200; 510-642-1823; FAX 510-643-5757.

The *EQUALS* programs, based at the Lawrence Hall of Science in Berkeley, California, have examined teaching strategies, from which they have developed innovative mathematics content to provide greater access and success for all students in mathematics. Additionally, the parent involvement program, *FAMILY MATH*, helps families become more positively involved in their children's mathematics education.

EQUALS in Mathematics:

- promotes awareness of equity issues, beliefs, and their effects on students
- promotes enthusiasm about mathematics
- encourages thoughtful approaches to mathematics, with good strategies and materials
- models classroom methods-group work, new assessment techniques, student self-evaluation, active and hands-on tasks—all to improve both adults' and students' mathematics understanding and attitudes
- increases awareness of career options and interest in math-related occupations
- supports change efforts to ensure that mathematics and equity interweave.

EQUALS INVESTIGATIONS, a publication for grades 6-9, includes some material for Spanish-speaking students. The five investigative units give middle school teachers and students opportunities to explore mathematics skills and concepts in familiar, sensible contexts. These four- to eight-week integrated units encourage sustained work that involves students in higher-level thinking, creative problem solving, planning, and communication. The students work together to explore problem-based curricula that are more in-depth than traditional exercises. Each unit has a range of entry levels that allows students of varying experience to be challenged on individual levels and to participate in group activities. The units integrate language, writing, and hands-on work in cooperative settings and can be used effectively in bilingual or multicultural classrooms.

Another gender-responsive EQUALS publication is *Math for Girls*. Designed to encourage girls' enjoyment of math, this hands-on curriculum challenges all problem solvers. *Math for Girls* is an eight-day course, with activities organized around five problem-solving strands: logic strategies, breaking set, creative thinking and observation, spatial visualization, and careers.

Equity Assistance Center, Consortium for Educational Equity, Building 4090, Livingston Campus, New Brunswick, NJ 08903; 908-445-2071; FAX: 908-445-0027.

The Equity Assistance Center for Region B (EAC) at New York University is one of 10 Federal Desegregation Assistance Centers covering Federal Region B (New

Jersey, New York, Puerto Rico, and the Virgin Islands). EAC has extensive experience helping school districts, especially those with diverse student populations, to address the many complex human relations issues that commonly arise. EAC staff works directly with district personnel to help them comply with federal civil rights laws and in addressing specific issues in race, gender, and national origin desegregation.

EAC provides gender equity services to school districts to improve curricula and promote equity in education opportunities for both female and male students. These services include assistance in the following areas: eliminating bias in student-teacher interactions, identifying and eliminating bias in curricula and instructional materials, creating bias-free multicultural curricula, achieving equity in school athletics, expanding career options for female and male students, identifying and preventing sexual harassment of staff and students, and developing/conducting programs for parents on gender-related issues.

Gender, Race and Media Literacy, http://websites.earthlink.net/~cml/index.html.
This site offers books, videos and curricula that challenge stereotypes, explore issues of gender representation, and uncover many multicultural perspectives.

Intercultural Development Research Association, 5835 Callaghan Road, Suite 350, San Antonio, TX 78228-1190; 210-684-8180; FAX 210-684-5389; http://www.idra. org.
Over the past 20 years, the Intercultural Development Research Association (IDRA) has established an impressive track record of success as a reliable, efficient and cost-effective contractor in the field of evaluation and research. IDRA's staff members' collective experience in training and technical assistance, evaluation and research has enabled it to develop a unique perspective regarding the evaluation and research needs of school systems and other public and private institutions. The IDRA Division of Research and Evaluation has extensive expertise in constructing evaluation and research designs, collecting information, conducting data analysis, and developing evaluation and research reports. Selected IDRA publications include The *IDRA Newsletter, Magnet Schools: Pockets of Excellence in a Sea of Diversity, Sex Stereotyping and Bias: Their Origin and Effects, Modeling Equitable Behavior in the Classroom,* and *Avoiding Sex Bias in Counseling.*

National Association of Independent Schools (NAIS), 1620 L Street NW, Washington, DC 20036-5605; 202-973-9700.
NAIS examines a number of gender issues that affect all levels of schooling for both boys and girls. One worthwhile publication is *The Great Balancing Act: Equitable Education for Girls and Boys* (1997), written by Anne Chapman. Maintaining that gender stereotyping limits both boys and girls, Chapman examines how to become mindful of gender stereotyping, and the need for equitable education for both genders. Specific topics in this worthwhile book include the curriculum of the real world, computers, athletics, leadership, and parents.

National Council for Sex Equity in Education (NCSEE), One Redwood Drive, Clinton, NJ 08809.

The purpose of the NCSEE is to provide leadership in the identification and implementation of gender equity in all educational programs and processes, as well as within parallel equity concerns, including, but not limited to, age, disability, national origin, race, religion, and sexual orientation. NCSEE is the only national organization for gender equity specialists and educators. It remains the voice for gender equity within the country and provides a national network for individuals and organizations committed to incorporating gender equity and reducing sex-role stereotyping. NCSEE members are a resource for schools, universities, community organizations, and policymakers who believe that equity in education means excellence in education.

NCSEE task forces include: Computer Expert Project; Curriculum Content; Health, Physical Education, and Athletics; International Issues; Multicultural Gender Issues; Sexual Harassment Prevention; and Sexual Orientation. NCSEE News Reprints include *Male Gender Issues* (1991), *Equity As Policy* (1992), *Sexual Harassment* (1993), *Restructuring & Gender Equity* (1993), *Computers and Equity* (1993), *Gender Equity in Multicultural Education* (1994), and *Equity Basics* (1994).

National Women's History Project, 7738 Bell Road, Windsor, CA 95492-8518.

This nonprofit education organization proposes to "write women back into history" and offers a wealth of resources for doing so: biographies; information on the accomplishments of African, Asian, and Latina women; calendars; posters and displays; and a wide array of classroom materials. Examples of useful curricular and instructional resources include posters, such as "Living the Legacy," and books, such as *Twelve Ways Your Group Can Support Women's History in Schools* and *101 Wonderful Ways to Celebrate Women's History*. The project offers *Women's Voices* (grades 6-12) and *Encyclopedia of Women in the United States* (grades 4-8). This organization also provides videos that focus on women and their accomplishments during various times in America's history.

Purple Moon, http://cnnfn.com/hotstories/busunu/9709/04/moon-ltr.

This San Francisco-based company, after researching gender differences and play patterns, has created two new games especially for girls. The co-founder, Brenda Laurel, found that boys like games emphasizing speed and action, whereas girls prefer being immersed in fantasy games that make them rely upon their imagination and their senses. Laurel also contends that boys want to achieve a high score and eliminate their opponents, while girls want to explore and understand opponents. Purple Moon has produced two new CD-ROM games, called *Rockett's World* and *Secret Paths in the Forest*, that fit with girls' preferences. *Rockett's World* is an emotional ride surrounding an 8th-grader's first day of school. *Secret Paths* is similar to a quest game, allowing the player to explore and find objects. Both games involve many plot twists and have multiple possible outcomes.

Search Institute, Thresher Square West, Suite 210, 700 South Third Street, Minneapolis, MN 55415, Tele: 1-800-888-7828.

The Search Institute offers a wide array of books, materials, and other resources (such as youth development programs) for helping young people. Selected titles include *Building Assets in Youth, What Kids Need To Succeed, Healthy Communities, Healthy Youth,* and *The Troubled Journey: A Portrait of 6th-12th Grade Youth.*

Tech Girl's Activity Book, http://www.girltech.com.

Today, technology is more accessible and easier to use than ever. As technology continues to evolve, it will play an increasingly important role in our daily lives. The majority of the "tech" products have been developed for and marketed to boys, however; girls tend to shy away from them. Girls who do not gain knowledge of and experience with technology will be at a disadvantage when they enter the workforce as adults, and society will miss out on the skills that many able females would otherwise give to the world. *Tech Girl's Activity Book* encourages girls to use different technologies, including computers. Each chapter includes sample exercises.

Professional Organizations

Association for Childhood Education International (ACEI), 17904 Georgia Avenue, Suite 215, Olney, MD 20832; 1-800-423-3563; http://www.udel.edu/bateman/acei

ACEI publishes *Childhood Education,* which contains articles on recognizing, respecting, and addressing gender diversity. Also, ACEI has published a revised edition of *Common Bonds: Anti-Bias Teaching on a Diverse Society* (Byrnes & Kiger, 1997), in which the contributing authors examine gender diversity and ways educators can build inclusive classroom environments.

Association for Supervision and Curriculum Development (ASCD), 1250 N. Pitt Street, Alexandria, VA 22314; 1-800-933-2723; FAX 703-299-8631.

ASCD publishes *Educational Leadership,* a journal that has long gained the respect of both practitioners and scholars. An excellent ASCD publication that addresses gender and other forms of diversity is *Educating Everybody's Children: Diverse Teaching Strategies for Diverse Learners.* This book is based upon the belief that differences in student achievement are often the result of differences in the quality of instruction.

National Council for the Social Studies (NCSS), 3501 Newark Street, NW, Washington, DC 20016-3167; 800-683-0812; FAX: 301-843-0159; http://www.ncss.org.

NCSS provides a number of worthwhile publications for middle school educators striving to provide gender-responsive educational experiences. First, NCSS offers "Social Studies in the Middle School: A Report of the Task Force on Sound

Social Studies in the Middle School." This detailed position paper addresses topics such as Students and Schools in the Middle, Social Studies Curriculum: Unifying Motifs, and NCSS Scope and Sequence Options. The paper also provides a comprehensive list of organizations and publications that contribute to social studies and gender equity.

National Council of Teachers of English (NCTE), 1111 W. Kenyon Road, Urbana, IL 61801-1096; 1-800-369-6283 or 217-328-3870; FAX: 217-328-9645; http://www.ncte.org.
NCTE provides a number of publications related to middle schools, young adolescents, and gender, including for example, *Just Girls: The Literate Life and Underlife of Young Adolescent Girls* by Margaret Finders (1996). In an effort to better understand adolescent girls' perspectives, Finders undertook a year-long ethnographic study at one midwestern junior high school. By tagging along with students to athletic events and malls, listening in on phone conversations, and observing them in the cafeteria and language arts classes, Finders gained a unique view of two sets of best friends—the "social queens" and the "tough cookies." Based on her observations, Finders explores how students embrace and resist particular social roles, how classroom participation is influenced by the underlife present within the school, and how social roles are defined and constrained by texts.

National Council of Teachers of Mathematics (NCTM), 1906 Association Dr., Reston, VA 22091; 703-620-9840.
An NCTM position statement calls for educators, parents, teachers, counselors, and administrators to influence the formation of students' attitudes toward, and perceptions about, mathematics. Crucial issues include: ensuring equal access to the world of mathematics regardless of gender, ethnicity, or race; offering the broad range of options available to students of mathematics; and believing that success in mathematics is more dependent on effort and opportunity to learn than on innate ability. NCTM contends that students experience the greatest developmental changes during the middle school years. Educators must continue to provide encouragement to students and enable them to develop confidence in their ability to make sense of mathematics. A focal point for this age group is making connections between mathematics and their future options, so that their academic and work-related choices are kept as broad as possible. NCTM offers a wealth of materials (e.g., *Mathematics for Middle Grades* and *IDEAS from the Arithmetic Teacher: Grades 6-8 Middle School*) that address students' mathematical needs.

National Middle School Association (NMSA), 2600 Corporate Exchange, Suite 370, Columbus, OH 43231-1672; 614-895-4730; FAX 614-895-4750.
NMSA has a standing committee on Diverse Cultural, Racial, and Ethnic Concerns, publishes multicultural education monographs (e.g., *Celebrating Diversity: Multicultural Education in Middle Level Schools*, which addressed gender and the need for schools to recognize young adolescents' gender), and provides profes-

sional development workshops on promoting multicultural education and an appreciation of diversity. A recent issue (May 1996) of the *Middle School Journal* that made notable contributions to gender focused on "Varying Views of Gender" and included articles on gender equity in middle school science teaching and on creating safe spaces in middle schools for the voices of girls and women.

National Science Teachers Association (NSTA), 1742 Connecticut Ave., NW, Washington, DC 20009-1171; 202-328-5800; outside North America, call 703-243-7100.
The NSTA catalog contains descriptions of more than 300 books, posters, software titles, and other resources that bring science to life. Publications from the NSTA catalog may be ordered from The Science Store at 1-800-722-NSTA. Examples of publications include *Middle School/Junior High School Science* and *Physical Science Activities for Elementary and Middle School.*

State Departments of Education

Steve Parham, Acting Director of Gender Equity Branch
District of Columbia Public Schools
415 12th Street, NW, Suite 1209
Washington, DC 20004-1994
202-724-4222

Jeannette Nobo, Consultant
Kansas State Department of Education
120 S. E. 10th Avenue
Topeka, KS 66612-1182
913-296-1978
http://www.ksbe.state.ks.us

Gloria Smith, Vocational Education, Gender Administrator
Louisiana Department of Education
Department of Education
P.O. Box 94064
Baton Rouge, LA 70804-9064
504-342-6259

Linda Shevitz, Consultant
Maryland State Department of Education
Equity and Assurance and Compliance Branch
200 West Baltimore Street
Baltimore, MD 21201
410-767-0433

Joyce J. Seals, Education Specialist
Michigan State Department of Education
Office of Equity
P.O. Box 30008
Lansing, MI 48909

Joyce Akeman, Supervisor, Special Vocational Services
Missouri State Department of Education
P.O. Box 480
Jefferson City, MO 65102-0480
573-751-8680

Sarah G. Hawes, Consultant
North Carolina State Department of Public Education
301 N. Wilmington Street
Raleigh, NC 27601
919-715-1649
E-mail: shaws@dpi.state.nc.us

Jackie Thompson, State Specialist
Utah State Department of Education
Gender Equity/School-to-Careers
250 East 500 South
Salt Lake City, UT 84111
801-538-7869
E-mail: jthompso@usoe.k12.ut.us

Darcy M. Lees, Program Supervisor, Equity Education
Washington State Department of Education
Old Capitol Building
P.O. Box 47200
Olympia, WA 98504-7200

National Resource Centers

The Center of Education for the Young Adolescent (CEYA), UW-Platteville, 1 University Plaza, Platteville, WI 53818-3099; 800-208-7041.
CEYA has files of information on middle level education topics of interest, such as ability grouping, advisory programs, after-school programs, at-risk programs, characteristics of middle school girls and boys, community involvement and service, exploratory learning, career education, and gender equity.

Girls Incorporated, 120 Wall St., 3rd Floor, New York, NY 10005-3902; 212-509-2000; FAX 212-509-8708; and Girls Incorporated National Resource Center, 441 West Michigan Street, Indianapolis, IN 46202-3287; 317-634-7546; FAX 317-634-3024; www.girlsinc.org.

Girls Incorporated is a national youth organization dedicated to helping every girl become strong, smart, and bold. For over 50 years, Girls Incorporated has provided vital education programs to millions of American girls, particularly those in high-risk, underserved areas. Today, innovative programs help girls confront subtle societal messages about their value and potential, and prepare them to lead successful, independent and complete lives. Girls Incorporated serves 350,000 young people, ages 6-18, at over 1,000 sites nationwide. Sixty percent of the girls the organization serves belong to racial and ethnic minority groups; 66 percent come from families earning $20,000 or less; and over half are from single parent households—most headed by women. Girls Incorporated develops research-based informal education programs that encourage girls to take risks and master physical, intellectual, and emotional challenges. Major programs address math and science education, pregnancy prevention, media literacy, adolescent health, substance abuse prevention, and participation in organized sports.

The National Resource Center of Girls Incorporated (NRC) is the organization's research, information services, and training site. Extensive research and evaluation conducted by the NRC provide the foundation for all Girls Incorporated programs. The NRC also responds to requests for information on girls' issues, and it distributes Girls Incorporated publications. Girls Incorporated's initiatives and publications include *Past the Pink and Blue Predicament: Freeing the Next Generation from Sex Stereotypes* (1992); *Girls' Bill of Rights* (1992); *Girls Re-Cast TV; Friendly PEERsuasion Program: Helping Girls Avoid Drugs and Alcohol; Preventing Adolescent Pregnancy; Sporting Chance Program Series;* and *Urban Girls Initiative.*

National Resource Center for Middle Grades Education, University of South Florida, College of Education, EDU 118, Tampa, FL 33620-5650.

This resource center provides a wealth of curricular materials and other information related to the middle school concept, such as teacher advisories. Books, teaching units, and a number of other materials are available that will help middle school educators address the needs of all young adolescents.

Youth Organizations

Girl Scouts of the USA, 420 Fifth Avenue, New York, NY 10018; 800-223-0624; www.gsusa.org.

The Girl Scouts of the USA (GSUSA) offers many services, such as:

- selecting girls for GSUSA-sponsored wider opportunities and providing travel opportunities
- acting as a link for the International Post Box (international pen pals)
- providing travel assistance, including information on traveling in the United States, information for girls traveling in Canada and Mexico, and cards of introduction for troops traveling abroad.

Publications include books, newsletters, and magazines for its membership, such as *Girl Scout Leader* magazine, as well as Girl Scout handbooks for each age level. The Girl Scout Catalog is filled with uniforms, books, accessories, and great gift ideas and items. To request a catalog, call 1-800-221-6707.

Women's National Book Association (WNBA), 160 Fifth Avenue, New York, NY 10010; 212-675-7805; FAX 212-675-7542; http: bookbuzz.com.

Founded in 1917 as a nonprofit, tax-exempt corporation, the Women's National Book Association is the only organization open to women and men in all occupations allied to the publishing industry: publishers, authors, librarians, literary agents, editors, illustrators, designers, educators, critics, booksellers, and those engaged in book production, marketing, finance, subsidiary rights, and personnel. The Women's National Book Association currently has active chapters in Atlanta, Binghamton, Boston, Dallas, Detroit, Los Angeles, Nashville, New York, San Francisco, and Washington, D.C. Readers wanting to join an association chapter should contact WNBA. Selected WNBA-recommended books for young adolescents include:

Babbitt, Natalie. *Tuck Everlasting.* (ISBN 0-374-48009-5)

Blume, Judy. *Are You There God? It's Me, Margaret.* (ISBN 0-440-40419-3)

Brink, Carol Ryrie. *Caddie Woodlawn.* (ISBN 0-689-71370-3)

Burnett, Frances Hodgson. *A Little Princess.* (ISBN 0-590-48628-4)

Burnett, Frances Hodgson. *The Secret Garden.* (ISBN 0-06-440188-X)

Creech, Sharon. *Walk Two Moons.* (ISBN 0-06-440517-6)

Fitzhugh, Louise. *Harriet the Spy.* (ISBN 0-06-440331-9)

Konigsburg, E. L. *From the Mixed-Up Files of Mrs. Basil E. Frankweiler.* (ISBN 0-440-43180-8)

L'Engle, Madeline. *A Wrinkle in Time.* (ISBN 0-440-49805-8)

Lindgren, Astrid. *(The Adventures of) Pippi Longstocking.* (ISBN 0-670-87612-7)

MacLachlan, Patricia. *Sarah, Plain and Tall.* (ISBN 0-06-440205-3)

Montgomery, Lucy. *Anne of Green Gables.* (ISBN 0-8125-5152-4)

O'Dell, Scott. *Island of the Blue Dolphins.* (ISBN 0-440-43988-4)

Paterson, Katherine. *Bridge to Terabithia.* (ISBN 0-06-440184-7)

Paterson, Katherine. *Jacob Have I Loved.* (ISBN 0-06-440368-8)

Spyri, Johanna. *Heidi.* (ISBN 0-06-023438-5)

Taylor, Sydney. *All-of-a-Kind Family.* (ISBN 0-440-40059-7)

Wilder, Laura Ingalls. The Little House series.

YWCA of the USA, 726 Broadway, New York, NY 10003; 212-614-2700.
The Young Women's Christian Association (YWCA) promotes health, sports, and fitness for girls and women. Health care is a primary concern of the YWCA (e.g., health instruction, teen pregnancy prevention, family life education, self-esteem enhancement, parenting, and nutrition). Operating out of thousands of locations in all 50 states, the YWCA represents more than one million women, girls, and their families in the United States. Globally, the YWCA represents more than 25 million women throughout 101 countries. The YWCA of the USA has been a supportive, institutional response to the changing realities facing women, girls, and their families.

Resource Organizations for Title IX

(Adapted from Women's Educational Equity Act's *25 Years of Title Digest,* August 1997, page 10-11):

AACTE Committee on Women's Issues
One Dupont Circle
Suite 610
Washington, DC 20036-1186
202-293-2450
www.AACTE.org

American Association for the Advancement of Science
1200 New York Avenue, N.W.
Washington, DC 20005
202-326-6400
E-mail: egavilla@aaas.org
www.aaas.org

American Federation of Teachers
555 New Jersey Avenue, N.W.
Washington, DC 20001
202-879-4400
www.aft.org

The Center for Law and Education
1875 Connecticut Avenue, N.W.
Suite 510
Washington, DC 20009
202-986-3000

Center for Women's Policy Studies
2000 P Street, N.W.
Suite 508
Washington, DC 20036
202-872-1770

Disabilities Unlimited Consulting Services
3 East Tenth Street
Apartment 4B
New York, NY 10003
212-673-4284
The Education Trust
Suite 200
1725 K Street, N.W.
Washington, DC 20006
202-293-1217
www.edtrust.org

FairTest
342 Broadway
Cambridge, MA 02139
617-864-4810
www.fairtest.org

Hispanic Policy Development Project
36 East 22nd Street
9th Floor
New York, NY 10010
212-529-9323

Myra Sadker Advocates for Gender Equity
Suite 300
1401 Rockville Pike
Rockville, MD 20852
301-738-7113
E-mail: DSadker@aol.com

National Association for Girls and Women in Sport
1900 Association Drive
Reston, VA 22091
703-476-3450
www.aahperd.org/nagws/nagws

National Association for Women in Education
1325 18th Street, N.W.
Suite 210
Washington, DC 20036-6511

National Coalition for Sex Equity in Education
One Redwood Drive
Clinton, NJ 08809
908-735-5045

National Coalition for Women and Girls in Education
National Women's Law Center
11 Dupont Circle, N.W.
Suite 800
Washington, DC 20036
202-588-5180

The National Council for Research on Women
530 Broadway
10th Floor
New York, NY 10012
212-274-0730

National Education Association
1201 16th Street, N.W.
Washington, DC 20036
202-822-7346
www.nea.org

National Women's Law Center
11 Dupont Circle, N.W.
Suite 800
Washington, DC 20036
202-588-5180
www.essential.org/afj/nwlc.html

New York State Occupational Education Equity Center
The Equity Center
8 British American Boulevard
Suite G
Latham, NY 12210-1402
518-786-3236
www.nysed.gov/workforce/equity.html

NOW Legal Defense and Education Fund
99 Hudson Street
New York, NY 10013
212-925-6635
www.nowldef.org

Title IX Advocacy Project
140 Clarendon Street
7th Floor
Boston, MA 02116
617-247-6722

Women's Bureau
U.S. Department of Labor
200 Constitution Avenue, N.W.
Room S3002
Washington, DC 20210
202-219-6667
www.dol.gov/dol/wb

Women's Sports Foundation
Eisenhower Park
East Meadow, NY 11554
800-227-3988
E-mail: wosport@www.lifetimetv.com
www.lifetimetv.com/WoSport

Summary

Providing gender-equitable experiences requires recognition and respect of girls'
and boys' differences. Educators must address all forms of gender inequities,
make the curricular content and instructional practices fair and responsive in terms
of gender, and change teachers' perspectives and practices toward girls and boys.
Being knowledgeable about and taking advantage of the available resources on
gender-responsive educational experiences can provide educators with a head
start to promote gender equity in middle schools. Undoubtedly, educators wanting to provide gender-responsive educational experiences for young adolescents
can suggest other sources of additional information. This chapter has examined
only representative materials. Other organizations, professional associations, and
state departments of education provide excellent resources that will help educators, both teachers and administrators. Advocates for young adolescent girls and
boys will want to seek other resources and materials that can contribute to the
goal of making middle schools gender-responsive.